THE DOCTOR DIGGER

THE DOCTOR DIGGER

LETTERS FROM THE GOLDFIELDS 1849–1860

EDITED BY JOHN M. RADCLIFFE

First published by Unicorn
an imprint of Unicorn Publishing Group, 2025
Charleston Studio
Meadow Business Centre
Lewes BN8 5RW

www.unicornpublishing.org

All rights reserved. No part of this publication may be reproduced, stored in a retrieval system or transmitted, in any form or by any means, electronic, mechanical, photocopying, recording or otherwise, without prior permission in writing from the publisher.

© John M. Radcliffe, 2025

The moral right of John M. Radcliffe to be identified as the editor and compiler of this work has been asserted.

Every attempt has been made to obtain permission for the use of the images in this book. Please contact the publisher with any errors or omissions for correction in future editions.

ISBN 978-1-917458-47-4

Cover design by Unicorn
Typeset by Vivian Head

Printed by Bell & Bain, Glasgow

Contents

Preface … 7

CHAPTER 1   Young Doctor … 10

CHAPTER 2   Voyage to San Francisco … 14

CHAPTER 3   Stockton … 35

CHAPTER 4   Fremont, Savage and the Mariposa War … 54

CHAPTER 5   Hopes and Disappointments … 64

CHAPTER 6   Australia … 72

CHAPTER 7   Doctor or Drugstore … 80

CHAPTER 8   Later Years … 93

Bibliography … 97

Index … 98

For Helen

Preface

The hero of our story is Henry Radcliffe, a twenty-nine-year-old doctor, who left Liverpool and everything he held dear, family and career, to follow the lure of the gold rush and the thousands who went to California in 1849, hoping to find untold riches in the remote reaches of the Sacramento and San Joaquin rivers.

In his letters Henry mentions several of his siblings and other connections, so I thought it might help the reader to know a little about his family background. In California and later in Australia he could not resist a feeling of nostalgia for the home he had left behind.

The Radcliffes were a Liverpool family. It would be strange were it otherwise, as the name occurs widely in south-east Lancashire as well as, curiously, in the Isle of Man.

Henry Radcliffe's grandfather, John, had left the family farm near Ormskirk and moved to Liverpool in the 1780s where he took up employment with His Majesty's Customs as a 'landing waiter', an official who supervised the discharging of cargo at the Liverpool docks.

John's son, Richard, maintained the socially upward trajectory by becoming an attorney (a solicitor in modern parlance). He was undoubtedly prosperous and, in due course, became the Town Clerk of Liverpool, the last such official to charge fees for his services rather than working for a salary. Richard was an early participant in property development. In 1840 he was behind the laying out of Hayman's Green, one of the most desirable parts of West Derby, in turn one of the more salubrious outlying suburbs of Liverpool. Richard married his cousin, Mary Anne Hayton, the daughter of an iron founder from Gresford in Cheshire. They had ten children, a number of whom died young, a not uncommon occurrence in Victorian times. Their eldest child was John, with whom Henry corresponded. John, too, became a wealthy Liverpool attorney. We will never know if there is any truth in the family rumour that Henry had fallen for John's wife, Kate. But gold fever, unemployment, love: any one of these motivations might have been the reason behind Henry's decision to embark on the *Ajax* in April 1849. One of his letters begins 'My beloved Kate', so who knows? Poor Kate died at the age of thirty-six in 1860. Her three sons, Tom, Edward, and Henry, were held in great affection by their Uncle Henry. John married, second, Emma Hughes, a redoubtable matron, whose photograph does not encourage one to imagine that she would have been very flirtatious.

Richard, the second son of Richard and Mary Anne, was also a lawyer but seems to have devoted most of his energies to property development in and around West Derby. Henry refers to his financial difficulties. This may be because he over-reached himself in his speculations. Pollard and Pevsner suggest that his developments in Stoneycroft (adjoining West Derby) came to a halt when 'the money ran out'.

Reginald, another brother mentioned in Henry's letters, was yet another solicitor, who also dabbled in property development. He was a renowned evangelist and famous for his oratory. He married an equally fervent evangelist, Jane Hunter. Henry took a tilt, in one of his letters, at what he perceived as a degree of hypocrisy in his brother and sister-in-law. He rails against 'the cant and humbug of religion' but at the same time we know he was a firm believer who delivered the occasional sermon.

Of Henry's younger brother, Charles (the nearest to him in age), we know very little save that he died at the age of twenty-six, leaving a widow.

The fourth brother was George, who comes in for some harsh

comment in the letters. He was regarded as the black sheep of the family until it was established that he was mentally unstable and his brothers arranged for him to be confined in Crichton Royal Hospital near Dumfries in the south of Scotland, an early Victorian asylum, where he lived out his days.

Henry's father, Richard, died in 1844 at the age of fifty-three. In a memoir, written at the behest of the City Council, his death is attributed to 'over-work'. Henry expressed concern for his mother in 'her many and sore afflictions'. We have no details of what he was referring to. It is possible that Richard failed to make adequate provision for his widow and daughter, Mary Anne.

Henry must have kept in contact with his family in England after he settled down eventually in Ballarat, as we know his son, Henry Hemington, spent time in England with the family pondering whether to train as a solicitor: a path that he ultimately chose not to take. Correspondence (if any) in the latter decades of the nineteenth century has been lost.

Thanks must go principally to the late Irene Radcliffe, granddaughter of Henry's brother, John, who preserved the Californian and Australian letters and ultimately gave them to me half a century ago. (This slim volume has been gestating for a long time.) Thanks also to my one-time secretary, Gilly Oliver, for typing my manual transcription of the letters, and to Sara Houghton and Sophie Cox for transcribing the final manuscript. I must also thank my brother, David, for the research he carried out in California and last, but by no means least, Ryan Gearing of Unicorn Press, without whose willingness to take on the project and boundless enthusiasm nothing would have happened.

John Radcliffe
London, October 2025

CHAPTER 1
The Young Doctor

This is the story of Dr Henry Hayton Radcliffe, the writer's great-great-great uncle. He was born while George III was still on the throne and died when Edward VII was king. He left Liverpool to seek his fortune in California in 1849. Success eluded him; he went on to Australia where he had better luck and where he died in 1903, never having returned to England.

Henry was at times an inspired letter writer and this book will include extracts from some of his most fascinating letters, both from California and Australia.

Henry Radcliffe (we will omit the Hayton in future; it was his mother's maiden name) was born on 19 October 1819, the third son of Richard Radcliffe, a prosperous Liverpool solicitor, who became Town Clerk of Liverpool. Richard died in 1844. Three of Henry's brothers became solicitors: Richard and John, his elder brothers, and Reginald, who was six years his junior. He was closest to John, to whom most of his letters were addressed. There was no medical tradition in the family but perhaps Henry took up medicine for fear of fraternal competition in the law.

He studied both in Liverpool and London. In Liverpool he was the pupil of Mr James Long, FRCS, Lecturer in Anatomy at the Liverpool School of Medicine. From October 1837 to August 1842 it is said that he 'diligently attended the Medical and Surgical Practice of the Liverpool Dispensary'. For the latter part of this period, he attended as an out-pupil at the Liverpool Infirmary. Subsequently he rounded off his studies in London at St Thomas's Hospital and other 'London Schools'. He received his diploma on 7 November 1843. He became a member of the

Royal College of Surgeons and a Licentiate of the Society of Apothecaries of London.

On the day he received his diploma he wrote to his father (care of the Town Hall, Liverpool) the following letter, which perhaps gives us an indication that his life was not going to be altogether smooth and trouble free.

> My dear Father,
>
> I expected to have taken my examination last Thursday but when Mr Power and his brother the Doctor gave me my final examination I was so unwell that they advised me to postpone the trial until this week and in the mean time to do nothing but amuse myself as they considered I had been overworked which I really believe was the truth for I was determined to leave no chance of rejection. I had a very agreeable examination and received my diploma but I am sorry to say that I have completely run aground in cash in fact I cannot say how my money is gone for I have only one pound in my pockets and I have a couple of weeks to account for with Mrs Lock so that I shall require not less than seven pounds to bring me home and settle everything here so that you will either be so kind as to forward a five pound note and Mr Lock will advance anything more I may require or send ten and I shall then pay his bill.
>
> You must excuse my running beyond the mark in this instance for the truth is I could not have left off studying without some excitement and that has been the cause of my present difficulty.
>
> Your Affect. Son
> H. H. Radcliffe

> **PS Send me the supply as soon as possible for I am very anxious to get out of London for I have nothing at all to do and I shall therefore be very uncomfortable.**

How many letters like this have impecunious students written over the centuries?

On his return to Liverpool the young doctor set about seeking employment. In January 1844 he applied for the position of Assistant House Surgeon at the Liverpool Workhouse (which embraced the Liverpool Fever Hospital). His application was supported by a number of eminent Liverpool medical men (possibly friends of his father), including his former teacher and mentor Mr Long (who was probably the family doctor). He was duly appointed and, in the course of the year, his title changed to omit the word 'Assistant'.

One wonders if absence from London softened his attitude to the capital. Maybe he missed 'excitement'. Whatever the reason in April 1845 Henry applied for the position of Resident Surgeon at the Bethlehem Hospital in London. His application was again well supported by worthy medical men but, in this instance, he did not get the job. He worked on at the Liverpool Workhouse for another year. On 25 June 1846 he attended to take leave of the Committee, his time as House Surgeon having expired. He left amid a flurry of accolades as to his diligence and professionalism, but one wonders why the young doctor's appointment could not have been made more permanent.

What Henry did over the next thirty-four months is not recorded, but on 15 April 1849 he boarded the *Ajax* in Liverpool bound for California. He was twenty-nine years old. He wrote a parting letter to his younger brother, George, then eighteen years old. George was a problem for the family as we shall subsequently hear. The letter reads:

Dear George,

I leave England in a few hours and cannot resist the wish I have to write to you; you must excuse the hurried nature of this communication. Now my dear Boy do work hard and avail yourself of every moment of your time – Not only to learn your trade but to gain information – If you had stayed at Holmes' industriously and had a good character I would now have found money for you to have accompanied me, but this is out of the question you will see when you reflect, that I cannot have any confidence in your knowledge of your business, which must be acquired before you think of leaving England or commencing for yourself, or do let me hear from my Brothers reports that you are progressing and obtaining a good character for industry and stability, then I have no doubt should the accounts of the Land I am going to visit be satisfactory that you, if it should be thought advisable, will come to me and you may credit me that I who have felt poverty and hardship will befriend and assist you in every possible way – So now my dear Boy do for your own sake – for me – for your Mother and also your elder Brothers, persevere in the right way and become a Man in every sense and meaning of the word – that you may do so and that I may hear of the same is the heartfelt wish of

Your affc. Brother,

H. H. Radcliffe
April 15th 1849, Liverpool

The references to poverty and hardship are possibly due to the difficulty in finding medical employment in Liverpool after he left his post at the Liverpool Workhouse.

CHAPTER 2

The Voyage to San Francisco

The discovery of gold, almost for the taking, in California in 1848 caused a lemming-like rush to the goldfields. When the news reached centres of population men dropped what they were doing and made for California. When sailing ships arrived in San Francisco crews deserted and made for the diggings. The port was soon clogged up with perhaps as many as 500 abandoned ships. We have no idea how Henry became the victim of gold fever. He may have heard of the five Californian trading and mining companies that were floated in London in January 1849. On the other hand, Henry may have hoped for better things than were on offer in Liverpool.

He was very fond of his sister-in-law Kate, John's wife. There is just a whisper in the family that he thought he might be getting too close. Whatever the reason, Henry joined the approximately 81,000 'argonauts' who had journeyed in hope to California by land and sea by the end of 1849. Most of these were Americans, the majority of whom came across the prairies, a journey of three to four months. Of the 39,000 or so who came by sea, usually via Cape Horn, maybe 6,000 came from European countries, including Great Britain. Henry was relatively lucky to be travelling on the *Ajax*. Many old hulks were refitted on the eastern seaboard of America for the purpose of the rush, and the ships were frequently ill found. Most of the immigrants complained of their treatment on the voyage.

It may seem odd to devote almost a whole chapter to a single letter, but Henry's description of events during his voyage to

California merit it. One has to adjust to his idiosyncratic style and ignore some of the archness ('thee' and 'thy'), sentimentality and lack of punctuation but there remains some fine journalistic writing.

Pacific Ocean July 13th 1849
Latitude 34.30 – 40 miles from Land 100 from Valparaiso
Ajax

My dear John,

My departure from Liverpool was on the 15th of April, fair wind, which afforded us a most delightful run to Madeira, which we reached upon the 24th – eight days sail – during this period I had ample opportunities of forming an opinion of all connected with the voyage – As regards Mr. Ward he promised a fine display of 'things for the inward man' for ourselves and friends upon the first day – alas they were 'no-where' cheese and biscuits with a few bottles of ale delt out with a most sparing hand. Consequently we were truly starved – I felt ill from down-right hunger; nothing to eat from early breakfast until eight p.m. fortunately you and Richard did not accompany us, along with the steam-tug – So ends with a couple of cigars and a walk on the poop the first day of my new existence.

I fancied I distinguished Kate – Richard and yourself on the shores of New Brighton waving a handkerchief as the last acknowledgement of separation – be this as it may – the thought pleased – even in imagination and ideality as well as reality has its corresponding pleasures.

> As slow our ship her foaming track[1]
> Against the wind was the cleaving
> Her trembling pennant still looked back
> To that dear isle 'twas leaving.
> So loath we part from all we love
> From all the links that bind us
> So turn our hearts where ere we rove
> To those we've left behind us.[2]

The Captain – I admire, a strict disciplinarian – upright and honourable – attentive to his duties – sparing of no physical exertion – exemplified upon all occasions for our safety and to the speedy termination of our voyage – he knows himself and what is due to others – He and I are good friends.

Passengers – a motley crew, of all shapes sizes and dispositions – generous mean – courageous – cowardly – thievish and blood-thirsty – a most wondrous lot 'The proper study of mankind is man' so says if I mistake not Pope – faith he ought to have come 'on ship-board' for three months and his inquisitive mind would have been satisfied – for here alone is man shown in his true colors – his virtues but they are few. Passions – vices and ambition, here (to the proving of the frailty of our kind) all – aye all are displayed.

The only one you can feel any curiosity concerning is Tom Beale – alias the 'Ajax fool' which cognomen he

---

[1] Henry has adapted the poem 'As Slow Our Ship' by Thomas Moore. (The poem describes the reluctance of a ship and its crew to leave their homeland.)
[2] The text in the original Moore poem is slightly different, beginning: As slow our ship her foamy track/Against the wind was cleaving.

has correctly earned from his vain boasting – drunken meddling propensities – easily imposed upon – generous to curry favour – despising all he fancies beneath him, from his assumed right of the character of a gentleman – leaving £300[3] per annum in the hands of his attorney – an incessant talker – Yet with all thy faults Tom I love you notwithstanding – honest – a firm yet dangerous Friend. –

We sailed on May eighth over the mystic Line, the scene of frolic and sailor-fun – Neptune with trident sceptre, grimly bedecked with bleached beard and wig of spun-yarn – with belt of tarry rope – 'How majestic is thy reign' How vast thy dominion How ancient thy rule – torches light thy visit with satellites hideous over the ships bows as she proudly cleaves the clear calm waters of the tropics – Thou departest in the meteoric light of thy throne 'Alias a burning tar barrel' Seen retreating on the still waters of thy domain – far far astern of the little world that renders thee homage – Mighty ocean grand and fearful even in thy smiles. –

You who live in the once 'Merry England' know not of heat, it is to you a vague and indefinite term – you conceive not the idea of laying barechested all about naked – with the boiling fluid oozing from every pore – to feel no coolness from the contact of water, except when dashed from a height – then it is delicious – to remain almost motionless on deck day and night – to search for some softer plank where to stretch your languid limbs – to watch the clear star-lit heavens – light as day – to see the same reflected below from the clear and transparent

---

[3] Approximately £35,000 in today's money.

waters – to feel no motion all calm – serene – still – ay profoundly still – tranquillity! Is it to comprehend Thee that miles upon miles are to be traversed, away away from land and the diminutive spot we call home? Yet thou too hast thy delights – The trade winds cease to fill our canvas, irregular in gusts and calms and veerings – farewell to sunny tropics, adieu to sorrow – Although I have lost a stone and am but a shadow of my former self 'faith, I could spare the flesh' – but not your smiling moons and gorgeous sunsets – the profundity of your contemplation – that teaches man to 'look from Nature, up to Nature's God' – The wind now is chilling at times and deceitful – We became conversant with it treachery by degrees – before it was a most obedient friend or rather anticipated our wishes, how very kind – it has changed now and earned the character of whimsicality like a coy maiden in her first love – or a starch prim old maid who knows not when she is well off – Keeping her suitors on the rack; learning what they would be at.

Well, Well, Wind with all thy changes, we'll round the Horn in three days and laugh in derision for thy abuse – Such were my thoughts one evening two hundred miles from the Cape and dashing the ash from my meerschaum I stamped the deck to send the blood tingling through my double stockinged feet, preparatory to turning in to roost – Sleep, sleep on – let thought rest – forget the past the morrow and the future – temporary oblivion-recruiter of our otherwise worn out existence –

Plaguing – very annoying – to be disturbed by jolts – by patients calls without the fees – still more so to be driven against a bulkhead and then forsooth out of the little thing they call a berth (sweet tiny berth I do love thee and prefer thee – (now I have built myself in) to the great spare bed with damask hangings at Eton Cottage[4]) Doctors are soon aroused, thanks to the hospital – what a din, cords cranking – wind howling, the dash of water over the deck, voices of Captain and sailors – Thank God no women or children 'Out out lend a hand'. Then what a sight, the beautiful white sails I have left double reefed two hours before spread to the breeze rent to shreds – A few hours hard work by the crew and about twenty passengers and the Ajax was under bare poles drifting like a cockleshell. Do you know what it is to be under bare poles for 48 hours in a heavy sea – blowing great guns – off Cape Horn with the wind right on your beam – the vessel drifting to leeward – the lee gunwales just above water – the deck approaching at times at an angle of 70 with an occasional sea coming over the weather side drenching you to the skin and then in the lurch or roll to windward the water recoiling and striking you just about the knees, flinging you on your back and leaving you to follow in its wake as the ship again heaves in the sea, you slide over the slippery deck at the imminent danger of breaking every thing that claims less thinosity [*sic*] than your own thick skull. No Land Liver you do not – Well I will tell you – You feel for all the world like a fish out of water – no doubt an uncommon sensation. If you essay to go to breakfast it is shoulder to shoulder – you try to get the tea to your mouth with one hand, the other clings to the table, then the ship gives an extra roll and away goes the provender like a dart and the plates dishes and

---

[4] Eton Cottage was John's home.

cups dance a jig or dash themselves most spitefully on the floor while you are crushed by the weight of eight fellows who sit on a form above, whose sharp bones or rough beards are certain to inflict anything but an agreeable acquaintance with your person – I 'dozed' till unmasked of belaying myself in conjunction with the youngest woman whose face and figure I could receive a squeeze from with a greater degree of pleasure than from those who dub themselves the Lords of creation:

During the storm we were driven two degrees out of our course in a North East direction indeed I ought to say 200 miles – in short we lost through adverse winds three weeks – the sport of the elements – wet and cold until we became accustomed or rather lost the hope of making a quick Passage. Fortune again favoured and how great a change came over the faces of all – no sooner had the breeze continued 12 hours than all were calculating upon the time of reaching Valparaiso. We rounded the Horn upon the glorious (to us) 26th of June going 10 knots an hour. The breeze continued until the 28th and we fully expected to reach Valparaiso so great was our luck in eight days. On the afternoon of the 28th we encountered a sudden gale or squall which came dashing the water to the breadth of ten miles into a cloud of white foam. The ship trembled heaved rocked and creaked and then a shock. I was standing on the windward side looking at the mighty waves – I called the attention of the Captain who, standing by my side, was giving his orders – to one larger considerably than any I had as yet seen, – on – on it came – I knew it would break and yet I was fascinated, I must watch and firmly clinging to the halyards I waited the shock – I who thought I knew the force of waves having so often watched their effects on the banks of the Solway had no idea of the power. The loud cry of the Captain, often repeated Hold on as he too stared into the face of the wave and then to feel the water above and around you – to hear the singing sound in your ears – to be in darkness to be sensible that with all your strength you are only able to hold on – your feet no longer on deck but hanging by your arms surrounded by water – all this is momentary, yet you comprehend it all – The wave has gone we are knee deep in water and our lee bulwark is washed away, the cook along with his coppers are in the lee scuppers with a couple of seamen and one passenger. The anxious and enquiring look which speaks more than words – is anyone gone? All hands on deck crew and passengers tumbled up and then the deck presented a fine sight stirring in the extreme – with the water knee deep. We were sailing under storm double reefed square sails, no matter their names as you are not a sailor –

These, everyone, gave way – or more properly the ironwork termed the barrel which fastens the yard to the mast broke in each, with the second foremast yard which with its sail was blown to leeward and hung suspended to the foremast. The sail was rent as you tear paper. The chain by which the yard is hung broke and was dashing to and fro each time it struck the deck a large link or two flew from the end – to the great danger of us poor fellows who were assisting the sailors to the best of our ability. The Captain after the storm in thanking the passengers for their exertions declared it was owing to the fearless courage displayed by them or he would have lost the whole of his sails – for we being on deck and having among us no less than four captains the sailors could go aloft, the work on the deck being done by us. Many have become familiar with the names of the ropes and all accustomed to assist in hoisting the sails indeed I am glad to say few betray any sign of fear or did not perform to the utmost of their power any work assigned to them. – To me the whole affair appeared grand – so sudden so unexpected so wild – it was not until from sheer weariness I sat down unable to do more – with bruised hands and torn face my body sore from the blows received from the jerkings of the ropes as we held on them in our endeavour to secure the wreck – that I could bring my mind to look upon it in any other light than a scene got up for our express amusement. To give an idea of the difficulty of holding even a small sail when it has once broke its proper fastenings may be conceived from the fact that fully twenty men had hold of the rope which brings the yard round – to the end of which it is attached – The object was to draw the yard to the deck – the whole yard torn sail broken ropes flying to leeward – a sudden puff of wind took the rope through their hands as if no force had been applied to it – throwing some on their backs and others of whom I was one upon their faces –

Pacific Ocean – man named thee so – only in proof that he in all he does loves to deceive – thy waters are the only ones that have come upon us without a proper warning – and yet I would not have missed thy raging billows – thy white foam thy howling wind – for

oh! There's a holy calm profound
In awe like this, that ne'er was given
To rapture's thrill;
'Tis as a solemn voice from heaven,
And the soul, listening to the sound,
Lies mute and still!
'Tis true, it talks of danger nigh
of slumbering with the dead to-morrow
In the cold deep,
Where pleasure's throb or tears of sorrow
No more shall wake the heart or eye,
But all must sleep.

LAND

The last appearance of the shores of Great Britain disappeared during the first night – then came the isle of Madeira – The wine press of Spain what association of ideas does thy sight recall – gloomy, yet withal sweet – rest in sweet repose. None who knew thee forget or cease to recall thy memory without a sigh – a monument more lasting than marble – adieu: Isle of England's mourn. –

Look there – at that large white mass that seems like a dense white cloud pregnant with snow – that is the Peak of Teneriffe[5] 12000 feet above the sea – its summit is visible covered with snow the base hid by dark clouds which clear away as the day advances and reveals the mountain in all its grandeur – The Landmark of the Atlantic – The resting place of the Eagles of the turbulent ocean from whose bosom thou projects till thy summit caps the clouds. –

---

[5] The peak of Teide in Tenerife.

Patagonia – or more correctly the isles of your coast is surrounded with – appear, while we are becalmed in the Pacific, covered with perpetual snow – we like not the vicinity of your iron bound coast and dread any further acquaintance with you and your gigantic inhabitants, farewell in gladness you, except England, are the only shores I leave with pleasure.

BIRDS AND FISHES

The sea-gulls we soon bid good-bye to – then come the flying fish chased by the dolphin – The whales in every direction – sharks with large black fins above water – Portuguese men of war – Porpoises black and large in great numbers. Mother Cary's chickens[6] – whale birds – these are seen in the Tropics – where we caught a shark and breakfasted upon his tail – The White Dolphin and Porpoise are seen at the Cape – Cape Pigeons very beautiful and tame – Cape Hens – the Huge Albatross of every colour – firing at them does not seem to startle them in the least if you miss they come within a few yards directly never altering their flight – The Cape Pigeon has been eaten and one passenger is very fond of them – They are caught with a line and hook as well as the albatross and booby. (A kind of gannet).

VALPARAISO

Landed on the 15 July being 90 days from our leaving England. The town is situated at the foot of a range of

---

[6] Mother Carey's chickens (a traditional name for storm petrels, that is, small seabirds known for their ability to fly far out to sea, even in stormy weather).

hills, in a slight bay, exposed to the winds and waves of the Pacific. The hills present a barren and desolate appearance being of a red hue with only a few patches of green. The lower part of the Town has one main street running from one extremity to the other it is here where the shops and the offices are and all the business of the town is transacted. The merchants live either above their offices or upon a high hill of difficult access by a rugged and tortuous path – The Peons and their families have their miserable dwelling upon the sides and tops of the hills, built without any regard to regularity or comfort. The sailors call the different parts of the town the fore top – main top etc. The manners of the inhabitants are very dirty – The women all smoke at all hours and spit upon the floor in every direction; they are also extremely ugly – married at 14y. or 16y. old shrivelled at 24 years – they seldom wash – fond of perfumery, to cover, I presume, an otherwise offensive odour – their food consist of beans cooked with grease and a herb which is used instead of tea, sucked up by a tin tube so hot that strangers are at first sight more or less scalded. – The country for 10 or 12 inland of Valparaiso consists of hills upon hills all barren except in some favoured spot among the rocks where myrtle-bay tree – box tree laurels of every variety – orange tree – wild potato – oat etc. are seen in [*illegible*].

We discovered on a shooting excursion a beautiful valley through the centre of which meandered a river – it resembled if viewed from the hills a tastefully arranged park, here and there beautiful trees in full bloom and all more or less aromatic – a few horses and cattle grazing

– above them a large turkey buzzard hanging on all but stationary wing ready to pounce upon his prey, so different from the flight of the large hawk. In this valley which we remember by the name of The Garden of Eden we rested our weary horses and no less tired selves as we had been in full exertion since 4 a.m. and partook of dry bread and cold water flavoured with a little brandy – this with the never to be forgot cigar constitutes a truly good and sufficient repast for the Hunter who were he to eat as we do in England would be overcome with heat and rendered incapable of further exertion – We spent the remainder of the day in the Valley where we killed three large foxes – these with an animal resembling a small tiger called the Chillian lion with the rat are the only wild quadrupeds of the country. Partridges snipe ducks – water-hens pigeons eagles hawks owls turkey-buzzards and a number of small birds with beautiful plumage are seen in abundance – They have no singing birds.

Mr. Brown received me very kindly as also a brother of Mr. Falkland, to both gentlemen I am much obliged. Mrs. Brown is expecting to sail for Liverpool shortly where no doubt Mr. W. Warrel will be apprised of her arrival. – Our vessel in consequence of having to discharge cargo will be detained two or three weeks in this port.

On my return from the country Mr. Brown with thoughtful attention handed me the united letter of my three brothers – for the kindness therein expressed I shall forever remain grateful but cannot allow my wants to trespass further upon those who have already done so much for me and I long to feel that total independence as far as humanity allows of its realisation which can only be gained by a man depending entirely upon the capability God in his infinite goodness has given him.

Reginald, will enjoy a pleasure in learning that his last letter was most amply appreciated and that the Doctor performed divine service according to our religion with either one of Blair's or the tract sermons or I am glad to say one of his own discourses – to prove the truth of the scriptures or to show the Godhead from the design of purpose in his works

> From Natures constant or eccentric laws
> The thoughtful soul this general inference draws
> That an effect must presuppose a cause
> And while she does her upward flight sustain
> Touching each link of the continuous chain
> At length she is obliged and forced to see
> A first a source a life a deity
> What has for ever been and must for ever be

Much good was done by the regularity of our service and I have little doubt that many a feud was prevented or staid in its course by the soothing and awing effects of our simple church service.

Richard – The progressive increase of his income so much surpassing his expectations affords me the most pleasurable feelings and he has my fervent prayers that he may have health long to enjoy and a mind so constituted as to feel thankful for the bounty allotted to him – in my reflective moments and they are many I have often recalled the past our boyish days our rise in manhood and although the study at times is pregnant in gall – yet there is a proud feeling associated with all its bile that I am one of a Brotherhood whose minds so opposite yet every one possessed of a nobleness of soul shining through every disadvantage and which will and has gained for them admiration.

George. No favourable account is conveyed to me regarding this poor boy. There are Peons here who sit at his age before the fire (charcoal) all day. They are like old or rather like their women and die soon – indolent – lazy – in a country whose riches abound – gold – silver – copper – fruit – plants – coal – all to be had for the gathering and yet they work not here too – did George now know his business properly (not like a Peon who when he can imagines he is a man or Carpenter) he without money or clothes would in a few years make a fortune not small – but large – English joiners have all left Valparaiso to go to San Francisco and the Masters with a few three parts educated native workmen or Peons are all that are left – they are absolutely coining money but the Masters are now obliged to work themselves because the natives are too indolent to learn more than rough work. Oh George George let a voice from the far far waters of the Pacific rouse thee to exertion and industry – let it sound the song of independence – let it breathe to thee of the sunny South – of trees ever verdant – of countries rich to overflowing peopled by men too lazy to gather the wealth spread before their eyes which requires the rattling blood of England to harvest – The Master Workman – the conquering perseverance – the bull dog courage. Have you these qualities George? if you have not – acquire them – at the age of 24 or 26 enter a ship as a carpenter – accept not a passage for then you would be lazy – come to these countries – where mechanics are gentlemen and great men – return in 10 or 20 years – buy a neat house at West Derby – call it <u>Independence Hall</u>.[7]

Mother and Mary-Anne – write to them of my whereabouts. Tell them from the hour I bid adieu I have experienced no illness no pain no anxiety – I have enjoyed feelings never felt before – the nearest approach to happiness – give my fondest love to my mother and may God in his infinite goodness console and comfort her under her many and sore afflictions.

And now dearest John, a few words to you and yours – first my little Tom – kiss him from Unco Harry and say, Unco will return one day or other when he is a man – but he must not forget Unco because he sees him not. – remember this John and do it. That should God spare me when I return old to view former places, I may have intercourse with the young who have lived with me in mind although our personal appearance is not known Little baby Ned – his mother's darling – too young to remember me although his dear smiling face will ever remain in my recollection. How pure and holy things are babies the cradle of the soul – destined for eternity – be careful of these little treasures entrusted to your charge and forget not that early impressions last. – Kate – often often you are before me with your smiling and sometimes would appear cross face – yes – we often laugh

---

[7] Underlining in the original.

together at my attempts to pin, sew and mend. Kate you have a noble kind – good affectionate heart – irritable at times granted – be careful then of my brother – he too is all in human nature you could desire – to do him all the loving heart of woman can do – Let him honour love and cherish thee as a treasure beyond price – and may in the lapse of time when the almond tree shall blossom and the whitened snows of many years be upon you – then may you be surrounded by those who honour and look up to you as parents and when the last solomn [*sic*] rite is over may you be reunited in those regions of bliss – of peace calm and joy when time is unknown – pain and care have no meaning there – is the fervent prayer to Him at whose feet the most humble may kneel, of your affectionate and remembering Brother

H.H. Radcliffe

Valparaiso
July 28th 1849

John Radcliffe Esqre,

Accounts from San Francisco are conflicting – upon the whole good – the port is crowded with vessels bound there filled with people – goods I fear will not sell well at present – your accounts in England are as good as those we get at Valparaiso and equally to be relied on – large fortunes have been made and the parties retired from business – Gardiner – South Castle St – did not send my shot on board – Richard will therefor take two pounds at least of his bill – he has also got several boxes of mine in his care – Reginald will call just to remind him to take care of them

> – Have no intercourse with Ward. When I write from S.F. I will inform you of his conduct at present it would not be politic although perhaps the newspapers may take it up.

Henry would have arrived in San Francisco probably in early September 1849, one of the very earliest of European hopefuls. His first letter from there has not survived even if it arrived. He says in his second letter (27 September 1849):

> My last communication you will receive in all probability subsequent to this as I foolishly entrusted it to an English captain of a vessel badly manned and who may never perhaps trouble himself with forwarding it to the proper destination.

By February 1849 the population of San Francisco was about 2,000. Throughout the year it was a feverishly active, growing town, though composed for the most part of frail wooden shanties, adobe huts and dingy tents. Henry writes:

> in haste before the opening of my novel residence of canvas walls, surrounded by men of every nation and of every grade. Most know not what to do, others are working with all possible energy.

> The population of the Town is upwards of 12000 which is changing daily from ships leaving for the Sacramento and from daily nay hourly arrivals filled with hopeful diggers – whose hopes and pent up excitement are alas too soon to be damped far below the cooling point, by the haggard and pale looks of some and the care worn features of all.

On arrival in 1849 he wrote to John:

> It is to be feared, from the most extraordinary artificial manner in which business is transacted here, that the apparent flourishing conditions of the colony will change and that the transition will be as rapid downwards for a time as it is has been upwards – Many have made fortunes and are retiring leaving their land and goods to be paid for by bills drawn upon fresh comers too ready to jump at any prospect for 'going a head'. The interest is most ruinous so that many pay 500$ per month for a store no larger than your dining room besides a very large deposit.

Henry must have brought a quantity of merchandise with him on the *Ajax*, hoping for a killing on a market crying out for goods of all descriptions. In this he was disappointed. Morell[8] describes:

> Goods were piled in great heaps in the open air for want of a place to store them. Commerce, however, was rather precarious for the fancy prices realised in the winter of 1848/49 led merchants everywhere to unload upon California any goods they could lay their hands on, however old and shop worn, however inappropriate to the conditions. Cargos were sold at auction; but in the end bales of goods were often used to make sidewalks or fill in streets, or left to rot.

Henry comments, 'Goods are exposed in every direction upon the ground with no covering but there is truly no stealing.' He continues (27 September):

---

[8] Morell, W.P. (1968) *The Gold Rushes*, 2nd edn, London: A&C Black, pp. 86–7.

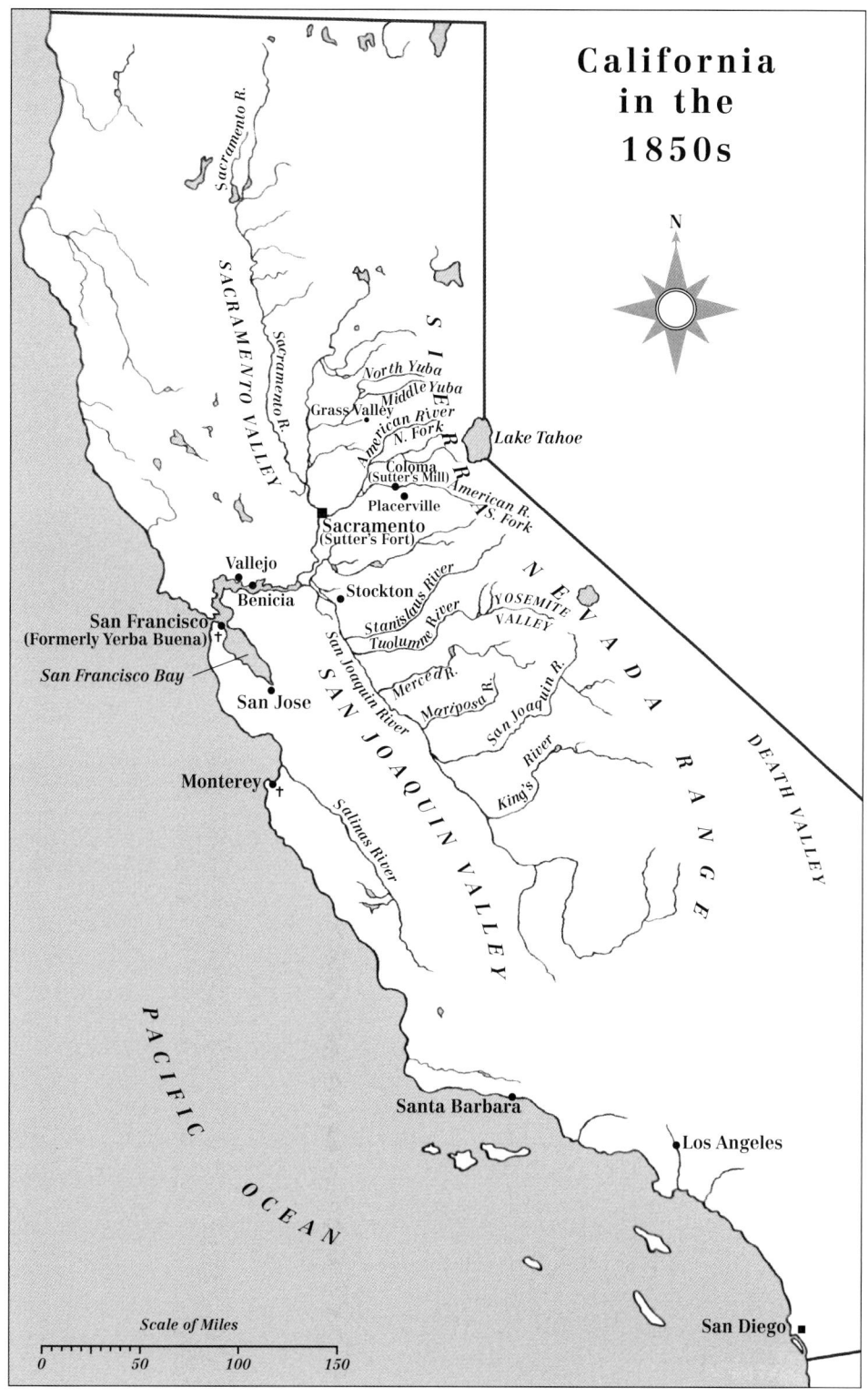

California in the 1850s. (N.Newton).

Abandoned ships at San Francisco. (Everett Collection Historical /Alamy).

San Francisco after the great fire of 1851. (Library of Congress).

Left, Mariano Vallejo. (Daniel / Oliver Galleryia). Right, John Fremont. (Library of Congress).

Clipper ship 'Comet' of New York in hurricane 1852 by Charles Parsons. This type of vessel would have been similar to the Ajax that Henry boarded in 1849. (Museum of the City of New York/CORBIS/Wiki).

Diggers. (Bancroft Library/Wiki).

Miner with shovel. (Collection of the Oakland Museum of California).

James D. Savage. Pioneer and commander of the California Militia, Mariposa Battalion and the first alleged non-Native American visitor to the Yosemite Valley. (US NPS).

Henry's brothers. John Radcliffe (left) and (right) Reginald, with whom he regularly corresponded. (Family Collection).

Enos Christman, Henry's typesetter on the Stockton Times. (Public Domain).

Stockton, 1849. Looking across the Stockton Channel. At the far right is Captain Charles M. Weber's Store and stern of the Susanne, a sailing ship that served as the first prison. (Pioneer Museum & Haggins Galleries, Stockton).

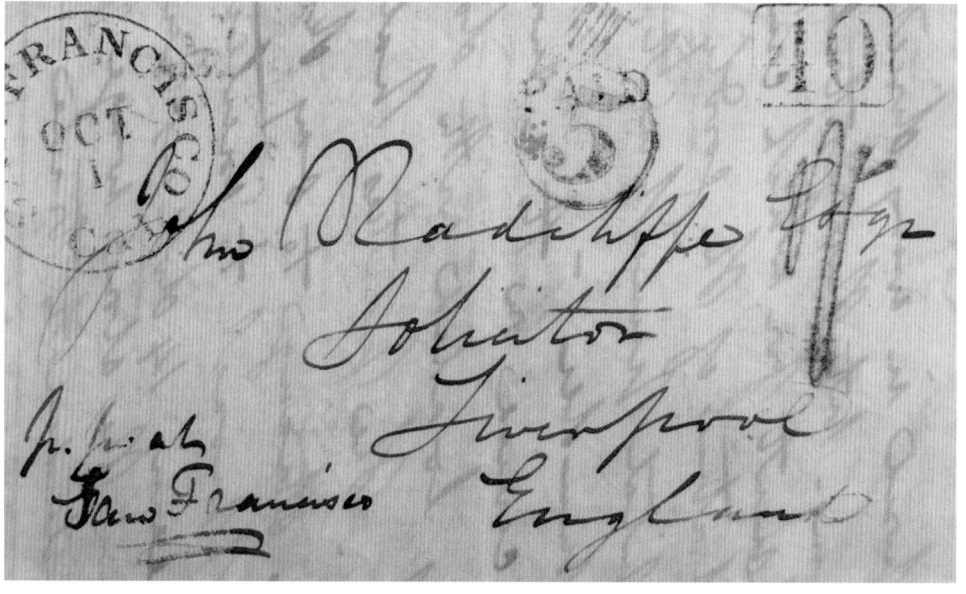

Envelope as addressed from Henry showing San Francisco postmark. (Family collection).

San Francisco May 30th 1850

Excuse this dirty paper it is the only one on the table and also the pile representation of San Francisco I send you as native as I feel assured you are never easy to see the news standing

CITY OF SAN FRANCISCO

My dear John

You must again excuse my non performance of my promise mentioned in my last. I am so fully engaged in our present exciting times that I have not had time to write fully as I really intended and wish to do this mail. —

The month of May commenced with a long tour over the Southern district of the Mines, the account of which I commenced in one of the papers, but owing to the disturbance in the Mines, it will not be continued as our paper is so contracted we have very little room even for the events of the week. It is impossible

One of Henry's original letters from California. (Family collection).

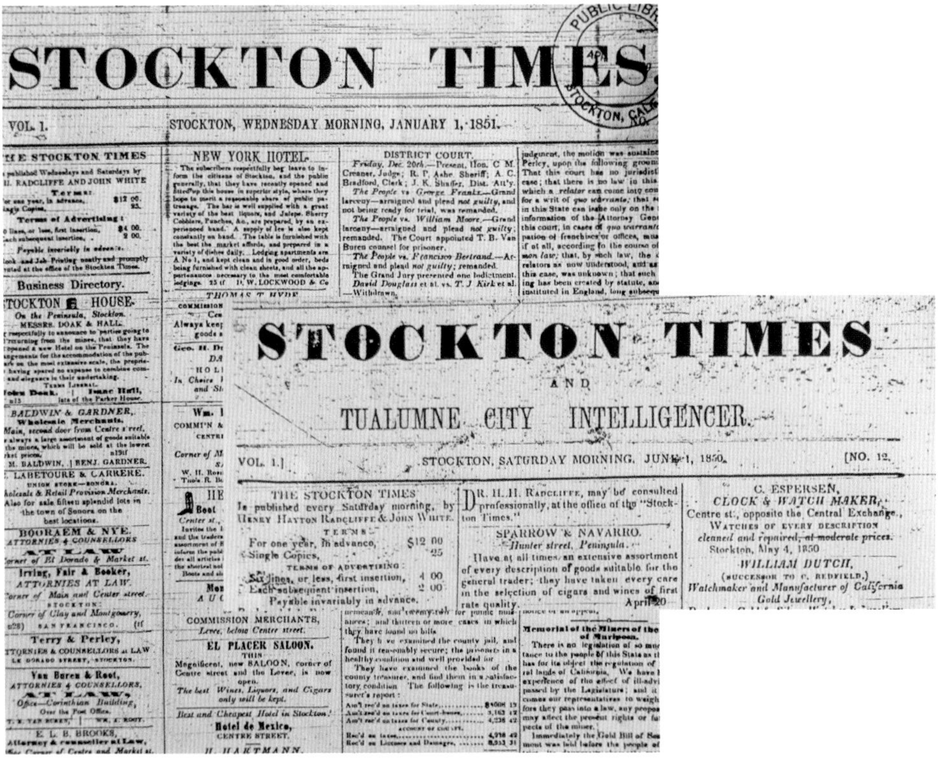

STOCKTON TIMES.

VOL. 1. | STOCKTON, WEDNESDAY MORNING, JANUARY 1, 1851.

THE STOCKTON TIMES
is published Wednesdays and Saturdays by
H. RADCLIFFE AND JOHN WHITE

Terms:
For one year, in advance, $12 00.
Single Copies, 25.

Terms of Advertising:
10 lines, or less, first insertion, $4 00.
Each subsequent insertion, 2 00.
Payable invariably in advance.

Book and Job Printing neatly and promptly executed at the office of the Stockton Times.

Business Directory.

STOCKTON HOUSE.
On the Peninsula, Stockton.
MESSRS. DOAK & HALL
respectfully to announce to parties going to or returning from the mines, that they have opened a new Hotel on the Peninsula. The arrangements for the accommodation of the public are on the most extensive scale, the proprietors having spared no expense to combine comfort and elegance in their undertaking.
Terms Liberal.
John Doak. | Isaac Hall, late of the Parker House.

BALDWIN & GARDNER,
Wholesale Merchants.
Main, second door from Centre street,
always a large assortment of goods suitable for the mines, which will be sold at the lowest market prices.
M. BALDWIN, | BENJ. GARDNER.

LABETOURE & CARRERE.
UNION STORE—SONORA.
Wholesale & Retail Provision Merchants.
Also for sale fifteen splendid lots in the town of Sonora on the best locations.

BOORAEM & NYE.
ATTORNIES & COUNSELLORS
AT LAW
Corner of El Dorado & Market st.

Irving, Fair & Booker,
ATTORNIES AT LAW.
Corner of Main and Center street.

Terry & Perley,
ATTORNIES & COUNSELLORS at LAW

Van Buren & Root,
ATTORNIES & COUNSELLORS,
AT LAW,
Office—Corinthian Building,
Over the Post Office.

E. L. B. BROOKS,
Attorney & counsellor at Law,

NEW YORK HOTEL.
The subscribers respectfully beg leave to inform the citizens of Stockton, and the public generally, that they have recently opened and fitted up this house in superior style, where they hope to merit a reasonable share of public patronage. The bar is well supplied with a great variety of the best liquors, and Juleps. Sherry Cobblers, Punches, &c., are prepared, by an experienced hand. A supply of Ice is also kept constantly on hand. The table is furnished with the best the market affords, and prepared in a variety of dishes daily. Lodging apartments are A No 1, and kept clean and in good order, beds being furnished with clean sheets, and all the appurtenances necessary to the most comfortable lodgings. 25 tf D. W. LOCKWOOD & Co

THOMAS T. HYDE

COMMISSION MERCHANTS,
Levee, below Centre street.

EL PLACER SALOON.
THIS
Magnificent, new SALOON, corner of Centre street and the Levee, is now open.
The best Wines, Liquors, and Cigars only will be kept.

Best and Cheapest Hotel in Stockton!
Hotel de Mexico,
CENTRE STREET.

DISTRICT COURT.
Friday, Dec. 20th.—Present, Hon. C. M. Creaner, Judge; R. P. Ashe. Sheriff; A. C. Bradford, Clerk; J. K. Shafer, Dist. Att'y.
The People vs George Frankz.—Grand larceny—arraigned and plead *not guilty*, and not being ready for trial, was remanded.
The People vs. William Moore.—Grand larceny—arraigned and plead *not guilty*; remanded. The Court appointed T. B. Van Buren counsel for prisoner.
The People vs. Francisco Bertrand.—Arraigned and plead *not guilty*; remanded.
The Grand Jury presented one Indictment.
David Douglass et al. vs. *T. J. Kirk* et al. —Withdrawn.

judgment, the motion was sustained... Perley, upon the following grounds... That this court has no jurisdiction... case; that there is no law in this... which a *relator* can come into court for a writ of *quo warranto*; that such... in this State can issue only on the information of the Attorney General... this court, in cases of *quo warranto*... pation of franchises or offices, must... if at all, according to the course of *common law*; that, by such law, the... relators as now understood, and as... this case, was unknown; that such... ing has been created by statute, and... instituted in England, long subsequent...

Memorial of the Miners of the... of Mariposa.
There is no legislation of so much importance to the people of this State as that which has for its object the regulation of the mineral lands of California. We have had experience of the effect of ill-advised... passed by the Legislature;...

STOCKTON TIMES
AND
TUALUMNE CITY INTELLIGENCER.

VOL. 1.] | STOCKTON, SATURDAY MORNING, JUNE 1, 1850. | [NO. 12.

THE STOCKTON TIMES
Is published every Saturday morning, by HENRY HAYTON RADCLIFFE & JOHN WHITE.
TERMS:
For one year, in advance, $12 00
Single Copies, 25
TERMS OF ADVERTISING:
Six lines, or less, first insertion, 4 00
Each subsequent insertion, 2 00
Payable invariably in advance.

DR. H. H. RADCLIFFE, may be consulted professionally, at the office of the "Stockton Times."

SPARROW & NAVARRO.
Hunter street, Peninsula.
Have at all times an extensive assortment of every description of goods suitable for the general trader; they have taken every care in the selection of cigars and wines of first rate quality. April 20

C. ESPERSEN,
CLOCK & WATCH MAKER,
Centre st., opposite the Central Exchange,
WATCHES OF EVERY DESCRIPTION cleaned and repaired, at moderate prices.
Stockton, May 4, 1850

WILLIAM DUTCH,
(SUCCESSOR TO C. REDFIELD.)
Watchmaker and Manufacturer of California Gold Jewellery,

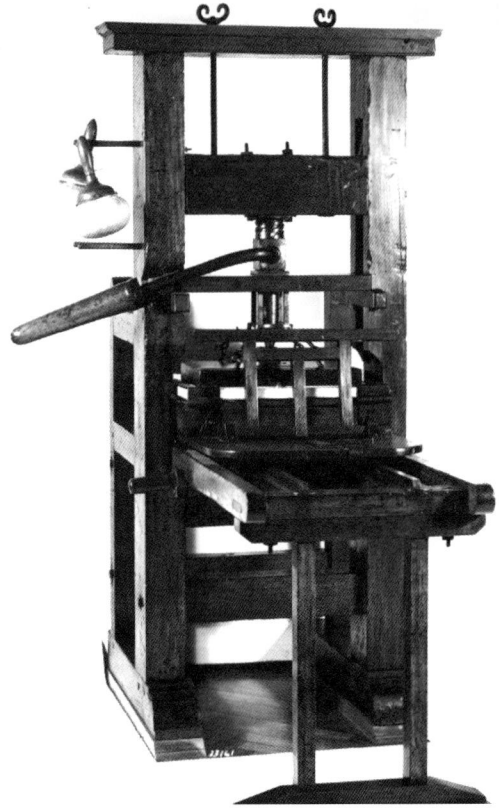

Above: Extracts and masthead from the Stockton Times newspaper, 1851. (Family collection).

Left: A one-pull Common press made by Adam Ramage. This would have been similar to that bought and used by Henry Radcliffe in publishing the Stockton Times. (Henry Ford Museum).

> I cannot speak favourably of the <u>Crates</u>[9] they are not even landed as I cannot find anyone to buy and I fear I cannot dispose of them to yield a profit however I shall consider myself as a creditor to the amount although prospect for goods is bad yet the accounts of the gold mines is exceedingly cheering.

Henry very soon developed a strong antipathy towards San Francisco.

> The Bay of San: Fran: is grand and would be really delightful were it not for the almost continued fog which seldom clears so as to reveal this large mass of water to its utmost extent. I am perfectly convinced that none can live for any long period in tents without the health suffering materially.

In rather prudish terms he adds

> Gambling is carried on to a most frightful extent over tables loaded with dollars, gold dust and bars. The parties habited as workmen and who, strange to say, display not even a remotest approach to excitement –

Henry quickly discovered that he could not support himself relying on his medical qualifications. In his letter to John of 27 September 1849 he says:

> I have done my utmost to get medical employment but it is more difficult than even in England.

---

[9] Underlining in the original.

For most of the forty-niners San Francisco was only a temporary halting place on the way to Sacramento City for the northern mines or Stockton on the San Joaquin River for the southern mines, a vast 'linen city' where in 1848 there had been a single log house. Henry had heard of these locations and realised the opportunities they presented. He chose Stockton.

CHAPTER 3
Stockton

Goods that did not arrive or, if they arrived, could not be sold were a continuing part of Henry's life. His early attempts to establish himself as a doctor were not very successful either. He did not immediately rush off to pan for gold at the latest discovery. So, what does an argonaut, with presumably a little money to invest, do on arrival at the other side of the world? Henry bought a press and started the very first newspaper in the town of Stockton. In January 1850 Henry, aware perhaps that a competitor was in discussions about starting a newspaper in Stockton, approached the owner of the *Alta California* newspaper with a view to purchasing their old press. A deal was struck, and the press was shipped to Stockton from San Francisco.

Henry bought an old Ramage press. It was a type of wooden, hand printing press designed by Adam Ramage in the early years of the nineteenth century. It was the first commercial printing press in California. Adam Ramage was a Scottish cabinet maker who had emigrated to the United States in 1795, settling in Philadelphia.

Carlo M. De Ferrari writes: 'The age of the Ramage press which came to California is unknown, but all accounts seem to agree that it had already seen extensive service and was well worn long before its journey around Cape Horn in 1833. Some evidence indicates that it was one of Ramage's earlier models, probably of pre-1820 vintage when press beds were still being made of stone.'

In a postscript to a letter to Kate dated 31 March 1850 he tells John:

I send you our first two copies – White I brought from San Francisco where the poor devil was driving a cart. He has served me faithfully for five months. In haste – my prospects are first class. I am the true proprietor of the Stockton Times, got through a meeting of many circumstances and the goodwill of my friends. It cost me before the apparatus was fixed $4,800 besides travelling expenses not less than $600. I have seen many hardships but never was unhappy. I have led a party from Stockton to Kings River or rather to the Mariposa. I have been reduced to a biscuit a day but was always contented ever since I left San Francisco. Whenever I come to that dreadful place I am ill so that I could not live here. People are never sick in Stockton during the summer so that I was obliged to invest my money in something to keep me or go to the mines.

Addressing Kate, he says:

Come with me to the office of the Stockton Times, a building 40 ft x 25 given to a Dr for one year by the Prefect: enter his room lined with linen, look at his little collection of books, withdraw that curtain and go see his bed made like a bunk on shipboard. Turn down that bear skin and see how the fellow lies. What, on deal boards with a blanket beneath him: true for he has lived harder and will from choice again, if God spares him, and again.

The issue of 1 June 1850 (published by Henry Hayton Radcliffe and John White just after Henry returned from another expedition) is called *Stockton Times and Tuolumne City Intelligencer*. This was a case of backing two horses. Things moved quickly in the goldfields and Henry and White were concerned that Tuolumne City in the heart of the goldfields would overtake Stockton in importance. It never did, although, again hedging his bets, Henry allowed himself to be elected an associate Judge of Tuolumne City in May 1850. By September, H.H. Radcliffe is shown as the sole publisher of the *Stockton Times*. In a letter to John of 30 August 1850 Henry explains what happened:

> I have been exceedingly unfortunate in the men I have employed and have lost no less a sum than £4000 from downright robbery and no hope of catching the rascals. I am not disheartened by the occurrence only thank my stars it was not worse. My first loss was through my agent MacKiernan, a Scotchman, sad rascals, the Scotch are everywhere. My next by Mr Eddy, a man I appointed because he was an Englishman. My next with the Alta California with whom I expect to get into law confound it [*No doubt connected with the purchase of the Ramage press*] and my last with Mr White who I took from a cart in San Francisco. In consequence of Mr White's conduct here I have withdrawn his name from the paper and sent him to Sonora where he is now working our press there with Judge Marvin. This man has rewarded me like a serpent rendering good for evil [*sic*].

In early June 1850 a superior printing press arrived at the offices of the *Stockton Times*. Henry and White had been planning to enlarge their paper. The old Ramage press was once more about to become surplus.

Instead of consigning the press to a well-earned retirement, the pair conceived the idea of establishing a new newspaper at Sonora, about 80 miles from Stockton and one of the latest gold rush camps, named so after their home town by the many Mexican miners who came to the San Joaquin Valley to look for gold.

The first edition of the *Sonora Herald* came out on 4 July 1850. It had actually been printed on the Ramage press back in Stockton and brought to Sonora on horseback by Enos Christman, Henry's typesetter. Christman brought out the second issue on 13 July on the old press, which by that time had arrived in Sonora. Enos Christman deserves more than a passing reference. He was one of the unsung heroes of early California. In 1849 the twenty-year-old Enos was an apprenticed printer in the offices of the *Village Record* of West Chester, Pennsylvania and engaged to be married to his sweetheart Ellen when he, like Henry, contracted 'gold fever' and, in July of 1849, headed to California, hoping to return to Pennsylvania with his pockets full of gold. Enos Christman's journal and letters to his fiancée back in West Chester give a vivid picture of what life was like during the gold rush. Enos failed to find gold in any quantity, although he travelled widely in the southern diggings, traversing all the major rivers flowing into the San Joaquin, such as the Tuolumne, the Stanislaus and Mariposa.

On 24 May 1850 his journal entry states:

> 'We are hard up, not having five dollars at our command, yet I feel nowise disheartened or discouraged, but hope to make a few dollars this summer. I walked into Stockton this morning and proceeded to the *Times* office. ... I asked for employment but they had hands enough.'

On 1 June he records:

> I walked into the city on Monday morning, hoping to get a job at printing or anything else, but found none.

> Business is very dull here.

He tried again:

> Feeling pretty well this morning, I walked into town in hopes of finding something to do, or purchase a scythe on credit. In the latter I was entirely unsuccessful. But in the former I was rather more fortunate inasmuch as one of the proprietors of the Stockton Times told me to come to work on Tuesday, as he wished to hire help three or four days next week, and intimated that it might prove a permanent position for me.

On 9 June he writes:

> On Tuesday morning last, I commenced type sticking in the Times office. Not having done anything of the kind for a long time, I feared that it would go rather awkwardly, but such was not the case, for I soon found my hands in and could set type as well as ever I could. … The foreman gave me ten dollars last evening at the same time telling me I could get nothing from the editor because he was lying in the sanctum, drunk. Wages here are fifty dollars per week, and I now have some prospect of receiving steady employment as they have purchased a new press and materials and contemplate enlarging their sheet in a short time.

He followed this up on 30 June with:

> During the past three weeks I have been steadily engaged in the *Times* office, working late and early. …

I am promised, by my present employers, a permanent situation after next week in the *Herald* office at Sonora in the mines.'

This took a while to come about but by 11 August 1850 Enos was ensconced in the 'offices' of the *Sonora Herald* and wrote in his journal:

On Wednesday afternoon, July 3, after having worked off the first edition of the *Sonora Herald* in the *Times* office at Stockton, the proprietor solicited me to take a horse and start immediately for Sonora, seventy-five or eighty miles distant, in order that the paper might be distributed. The day after my arrival I distributed copies of the first number of the *Herald* throughout the town. On the following day I bought lumber, borrowed a saw and hatchet, and fitted up some 'stands' in a tent which we use for an office. I have known of printing offices in log cabins with the latchstring always hanging out, but here, I am seated at a table covered with papers in the middle of a 'rag house,' ten by fourteen feet, surrounded by all the paraphernalia of a printing establishment. When I speak of printing materials, I do not mean that we have such an assortment of things as we had in the *Record Office.* On the contrary, we have but two or three cases of old type, a wooden 'stick' manufactured by my own hands with a jackknife, and an old Ramage press that has long been a pioneer in the business, the first numbers of nearly all the papers now printed in California having been printed upon it after it had been brought second-hand from the States through Mexico: 1st, the paper at Monterey; 2d, *Alta California*, San Francisco; 3d, *Placer Times*,

Sacramento City; 4th, *Times*, Stockton; and lastly, the *Sonora Herald*. It well deserves the title of the 'Pioneer Press.' It has spoken to millions and no one can calculate the amount of good it has already done, nor estimate what amount it is yet capable of doing. It has already crossed the continent in its mission of good from the Atlantic shores to those of the Pacific, and is now on its way back. I doubt not but it will next be heard from on the summit of the Sierra Nevada range, and hope it will continue in its course until it is met on the broad plains by something from the East. Then as a reward for past services, it well deserves to be placed by the side of Franklin's old press in Washington as a curiosity for the future generations to look upon. In a century to come when our children have read the history of California, with what wonder would they look upon that press. It has escaped many dangers, fire and shipwreck, and when its labours are over, I trust it will receive an eulogy worthy of the subject.

There is a degree of uncertainty about exactly who were the proprietors of the *Sonora Herald* and in what proportion. Henry, in his letter of 30 August 1850 quoted above, uses proprietorial language. As we have read, the Ramage press was purchased by Henry in the first instance, but if White became his partner, he would no doubt have acquired a share in it. The issues of the *Sonora Herald* of 27 July and 3 August show the proprietors as H.H. Radcliffe, J.G. Marvin and John White. However, the issue of the *Stockton Times* of 21 September 1850 notes that Dr Radcliffe had disposed of his interest in the *Sonora Herald*. This may have come about as a result of a series of rather inconclusive lawsuits. It appears that Henry and White borrowed money from Judge James R. Reynolds in order to get the *Sonora Herald* under way. By September 1850 Reynolds was getting impatient about getting his money back and had a writ of attachment served on the offices of the *Sonora Herald*. Marvin also owed a considerable sum to Reynolds. White transferred his interest in the paper to Reynolds and, as noted in Enos Christman's journal, 'with his lady vamosed for Stockton in the stage' (8 September). Back in Stockton a forgiving Henry Radcliffe allowed him to resume his position at the helm of the *Stockton Times*. There is nothing to show that Henry settled with Reynolds in the same manner, but assumptions can be made. It would appear that Reynolds then had a half share in the paper with Marvin holding the other half. Poor Enos was left poorer to the tune of $467 in unpaid wages ('they have promised me money every day for a week'). Worse was to follow. His journal entry for 22 October records:

> **About ten days since, the *Sonora Herald* died, that is, became defunct for want of patronage, and consequently my employment ceased. The proprietors, not being able to hand over the dust, gave me their notes for five hundred dollars, but I fear I shall not be able to collect the money I have earned.**

In the event Enos Christman went gold digging (not very successfully) for a couple of weeks before the *Sonora Herald* was resuscitated by Judge Marvin and Dr Lewis C. Gunn, who had acquired Judge Reynold's share, on 5 November and Christman started 'sticking type' again. A few weeks later Christman purchased one half of the *Sonora Herald* from Judge Marvin in settlement of the wages he was owed. Under Dr Gunn and Christman the *Herald* finally became firmly established. Enos Christman eventually sold out, as his journal entry of 9 August 1851 records: 'I have sold out my interest in the Herald at a fair price and am now permanently engaged as printer and Deputy Recorder at a salary sufficient to save over one hundred dollars per month.' He left Sonora on 21 June 1852, arriving back in New York on 23 July. He married his fiancée Ellen who had waited faithfully for him for three years.

The *Stockton Times* had a competitor in the shape of the *Stockton Journal*, which was started by John Robb in June 1850. This gentleman was unashamedly Republican in his sentiments whereas the *Stockton Times* had declared itself apolitical. There was plenty of printing work to be had initially and the *Stockton Times* did most of the printing work for the city, but when in early 1851 Robb was elected as a member of Stockton City Council, he organised it so that all civic printing work went to the *Journal*.

The *Stockton Times* may have lamented over the death of democracy, but this was a serious blow. Henry and White then lost their principal printer, Mr Byron Gallup, to the *Journal*. On 20 January 1851 Henry complains to John:

> **We can only afford for the last month to pay our men $30 a week and this week I don't believe we shall reach that sum – Printers wages are too high and I hope will be reduced.**

Given that Henry, who by this time was spending long periods on expeditions to remote mining areas or looking after his patients in the hospital, seems to have lost interest in his paper it is not surprising that the newspaper folded. On 26 April 1851 the *Stockton Times* issued a valedictory:

> **With the present number will cease our connection with this newspaper. A Democratic organ, of a larger size, will be issued under another name on Wednesday next. We take this opportunity of briefly thanking our friends for**

their kind encouragement rendered to us through a period of 14 months. We hope that we have left our mark for good upon our adopted city. – Through ill report and good report, we have honestly done our duty, nothing extenuating nor setting down aught in malice; and we have watched, with the deepest interest, the social and commercial progress which has been made by this community.

May the old press flourish in the midst of its new duties as greatly as our wishes may picture. *Vivat in eternum*[10]

The present current advertisements will be continued in the new journal until ordered to be withdrawn.

We know nothing of the successor paper. Suffice it to say that Henry had no interest in it. By now he was devoting his time to prospecting in the remote valleys of the Mariposa Creek (then called the Mariposa River) and the Kings River, even further south.

Henry really could not resist the temptation to go on expeditions. In his time in California he completed at least four. When he really should have been attending to the affairs of the *Stockton Times*, the *Sonora Herald* or the Stockton Hospital he was away in the farthest reaches of the San Joaquin Valley or in the remotest heights of the Sierra Nevada. In the winter months following his arrival in San Francisco he 'led a party from Stockton to Kings River or rather to the Mariposa'. Later that year (30 August), when excusing himself from failing to write, he says, 'I do not think I have missed one month except when I was on an expedition to the headwaters of the San Joaquin.'

During this first expedition Henry established a trading post at the Mariposa but as we will read the individual who had charge

---

[10] *Vivat in aeternum* is a Latin phrase meaning 'May it live forever'.

of his tent let him down to the tune of $2,000 in gold dust. In his letter of 26 April 1850, Henry, ever footloose, says, 'I should have left tomorrow morning for a tour through the mines to establish agents at the numerous solicitations of my friends.' His departure was delayed but he later reports, 'The month of May commenced with a long tour over the southern district of the mines.' This trip gave rise to a most enthusiastic report in a letter to John of 31 May 1850, sent from San Francisco:

> I may mention in proof of the extraordinary healthfulness of our climate in the great Valley of the San Joaquin that for twenty nights prior to my arrival here I have slept in the open air with a horse rug for my covering our camps have been on the open plain – banks of rivers and mountain tops. The mines of California are in truth inexhaustible – ranges of quartz impregnated with gold exist which would take 1000 years to work if the whole of the Californian population were concentrated upon the spot with competent machinery. Cinnibar in endless quantities – iron – silver I have specimens from the localities I have visited – All accounts in our paper are strictly true and you may fully rely upon any future accounts we may publish. You will forgive me for this letter as I am so hurried to attend a meeting which I cannot neglect and for which I left Stockton immediately on my return from the mines.

Maybe the affairs of the *Stockton Times* and the *Sonora Herald* kept him in Stockton for the next six months, as the next expedition we hear of is not until March 1851. He writes to John on 1 April 1851:

> I returned a few days ago from my expedition to the

mountains our object was to discover and claim gold quartz veins and we have been perfectly successful. The company in Stockton on my return cannot agree as to the shares to be taken by each party and they are now in dispute. I told them plainly if they did not agree I would leave them *instanter* and 'go on my own hook' they have not as yet decided and in accordance with my determination I vamose [*sic*] tomorrow morning for the mountains. I have my own followers and am perfectly aware of a good locality both for placer (i.e panning) and quartz mining. My plan is to employ Mexicans after the placer is properly opened, to sink shafts and explore the quartz vein so that the product of the placer may pay their wages by which means the extent of my loss can only be the time occupied in exploring.

The same letter reports:

During my late trip we discovered a rich silver vein which would supply a quantity of metal as great as all the gold put together in California – it would be absurd for me to say the quantity lying uncovered on the earth – if it was not for the verification of others the statements would not be credited here far less in England. California is one mass of mineral wealth. Strangers to 'prospecting' always doubt because only small specimens of the ore are brought down – they think among such treasures why not bring down a large quantity – now the reason is this, a small horse has [to] carry in my person say 185 lbs [*about 13 stone*] then blanks – rifle balls – pistols – hammer crowbar and pick with shovel and bowl – then he gets a mighty little grub sometimes we pack barly also –

well everyone knows that – although we do not like it to be known – we may have to run either from Indians or what is worse a grisly – and the less weight we can do with the safer we are – Among our luck we found a mountain with a vein of white sand running directly through it about 10 feet wide having decayed quartz in its centre – the sand we washed and found it to pay six bits to the pan (60c) we dug into the sand and its richness was uniform – situation near Aqua Fria – quartz veins exist in every direction for the extent of 30 miles south 8 north of this point and I am not prepared to say they are all gold bearing or that they are so rich as to pay but many of them present gold to the naked eye and will average from 50 cents to a 100 cent per pound.

Palmer and Cooks vein averages 50 cents – the pockets increases this average – their profit is $600 per diem with crushers of 130 lbs 12 in number and steam power of 8 horse their works are very incomplete but they avail themselves of every opportunity to improve. Their claim is situated at Mariposa on Col. Fremonts claim who however will never be able to hold indeed he has no title I am firmly of the opinion that the working of quartz will be believed by most parties now engaged to prove a failure – this will arise from the very imperfect adaptation of machinery to extract the gold. Palmer and Cook are aware that they loose [sic] more than one third of the gold because their stamps are incapable of pounding the quartz to a powder sufficiently fine for the action of mercury.

Back in San Francisco on 14 May 1851, having lost everything in the fire that destroyed Stockton on 6 May of that year, he writes to Kate that while in the mountains of the Sierra Nevada he had a return of fever with delirium. This was a recurrence of an illness he had had the previous year, but worse, and his companions decided to provide for his removal back to Stockton. He had been ill for a couple of weeks. It seems that this may have put him off further expeditions for such letters as we have for later in 1851 make no reference to such activities.

As if what with publishing, doctoring, gold prospecting and performing quasi-judicial duties in Tuolumne, Henry did not have enough to do, he found time to get involved with matters ecclesiastical. He came from a family with strong, if non-conformist, religious views. His grandfather had been a church warden of St James's Church in Liverpool with W.E. Gladstone's uncle, and his brother Reginald was one of the outstanding evangelistic orators of the nineteenth century. Henry's view of his brother was that he was a 'fanatic', and possibly a bit of a hypocrite. Clearly Henry was not averse to taking the odd drink. His doctor in Liverpool, Dr Long, had been worried that Henry was drinking too much, but in a letter to John on 20 January 1851 Henry says:

> **Please send them [two pieces of gold] to Long with my best wishes and these words 'avoid fuddling' and say I am not yet addicted to <u>drink</u>[11] according to his opinion his prognostics are most entirely wrong as regards me I grow no stouter and have none of the complaints he used to trouble me with.**

Reginald appears to have been strictly teetotal. His attitude vexed Henry especially when he heard that Emma Lindley (a 'warm hearted good piously disposed girl') had been judged 'too bad' to be present at Reginald's marriage. He wanted the ornament he was sending to be worn by someone who had the courage to be

---

[11] Underlining in the original.

pious 'without <u>the cant and humbug</u> of <u>religion</u>'.

Despite these robust views on religion Henry became involved with the Methodist Church in Stockton. The Methodists formed the first church in Stockton. It was inaugurated on 16 March 1850, one day ahead of the Presbyterians. Henry became one of the first Trustees and was not averse to preaching the odd sermon.

Henry was endlessly hopeful that his medical practice would expand. As early as June 1850 the *Stockton Times* carried a small advertisement to the effect that:

> **Dr H.H. Radcliffe may be consulted professionally at the office of the *Stockton Times*.**

By August he was advertising a 'Private Hospital' on El Dorado Street where the physicians attached were himself and a Dr William Simpson.

On 30 August 1850, in a letter from Stockton, Henry tells John:

> **I flatter myself that I am considered the first medical man here and I may say my practice increases; but we have so little sickness that it is not worth consideration, what with horses and help all profit 'vamoses'.**
>
> **It is only operations that pay – so hurrah for shooting but unfortunately these Colts kill the man at once for if the first shot does not kill a second will do the business I give you a drawing of one of the 'Colts' they are without doubt the most murderous weapons invented and when accustomed to their use a man is certain of from 30 to 80 yards.**

In the same letter Henry adds:

> For the last four months the best mining period of the year we have – trade has been at a complete standstill and no 'oro' to be had – at one period as many as seven murders or 'Killings'a day and no punishment awarded. The occasion of the disturbance was the injudicious tax upon foreigners of $20 per month.

By the October of 1850 Henry and a French Dr Lavignes had set up the Stockton Hospital on the corner of Center and Market Street. Dr Simpson seems to have faded from the picture.

Henry soldiers on against the odds. In a letter dated 20th January 1851 he explains to John:

> When I took the Hospital I gave up my Editorship of the paper and White (who I cannot get rid of) came from Sonora.

And later in the same letter:

> I opened an Hospital and had it filled with patients from $10 to 8 per diem, this lasted for six weeks and yielded a handsome profit but now the winter being so healthy I have not a single patient – no not one, all gone like the contents of my pockets".

Echoes of the impecunious student doctor.

Henry found that he could not rely on 'medical employment'. He may have founded the first hospital in Stockton but, as he reported to his brother, 'all profit vamoses'. Henry did, however, describe in considerable detail an operation he had carried out. In a letter to John dated 1 April 1851 he writes:

No medical practice in Stockton or indeed in California at the present season of the year not a single case of sickness except gunshot wounds or accidents which I am more likely to meet with in the mines than here. I performed my great operation a few days since the second after my arrival from the mines a poor fellow Capt. Adams received accidentally a gunshot wound in the hip making an aperture of the size of a dollar and splintering the femur to the hip joint immediate amputation was decided upon which I performed as soon as reaction had taken place I was only about two minutes in the operation – tying arteries etc. Chloroform ether had against my opinion and also Dr Brown from Scotland been administered the man became perfectly insensible from which state he never recovered. The operation was performed by introducing the knife from the anterior part of the thigh about 15 lines from the (ante superior spinous [*illegible*] of the ileum) front part of the hip bone passing it directly downwards and backwards external to the head of the femur to the tuber ischia (or seat bone) from which points I cut downwards and onwards to the margin of the external wound thus forming my external flap.

I then tied the divided arteries and formed the internal flap by passing the knife from below upwards to the point of introduction and cutting downwards and inwards to the extent of six inches seizing the divided femoral artery with finger and thumb of my left hand – by this precaution my poor patient did not loose [*sic*] two ounces of arterial blood I am happy to say it was the decided opinion of the surgeons and non-professional parties present that the man died from the effect of chloroform.

> I experienced no difficulty in the dislocation of the head of the thigh bone and I feel confident that I could perform the same operation in less time that the average time occupied in amputation of the femur by our English surgeons this is a bold operation – but a man acquires coolness and firmness such as is seldom gained even among your hospital surgeons in England.

He also recounted in a letter dated 26 April 1850 to John:

> I would have taken Kate with me up the river of Butterflies, my Mariposa, we would have spoken with the man I visited there in the winter – he suffering from frost bite long suffering, now a cripple for life 'on dit' his life is due to me.

Henry eventually gave up trying to make a go of doctoring in California. He wrote to Kate from San Francisco on 30 June 1851:

> Since the time in Stockton I came to San Fran and collected debts to about $2000, opened a little doctor's store in Kearney St when I was gradually forming a connection when the streak of bad luck continued and last fire completely determined me never to hold a cent's worth of burnable property in California so dear Kate after two fires following one upon the other you will think I am much dispirited in which I assure you you are mistaken for I am just as happy and contented and equally as positive of making a fortune that is enough for a gentleman to live on, as ever; indeed I am really rejoiced

that the last fire did up the doctor's stuff for it is the last I shall have to do with Physic a thing I most hate, and a complete drug store costs a great deal of money in this country.

This resolve held until his latter years in Australia. Doctoring or no, Henry's fortunes fluctuated and with them his spirit.

CHAPTER 4

Fremont, Savage and the Mariposa War

In 1846 when the white population of California was minimal (mainly consisting of people of Spanish/Mexican descent) there were perhaps 150,000 Indians subsisting quietly, divided into numerous scattered tribal groupings. In the main they lived harmoniously. There was little or no empire building, as there was more than enough land, game, fish and natural products to satisfy them all. The discovery of gold and the arrival of the forty-niners devastated their way of life. With chilling inevitability, over the next twenty-five years or so California's Indian population was reduced to a mere 30,000, the survivors taking refuge where they could, in the most inhospitable parts of the state, infertile desert areas and the Sierra Nevada mountains. Sickness and falling childbirth must have played a part but in the main it was casual (and sometimes organised) killing that reduced their number. The campaigns against the Indians (and campaign is too kind a word for the small hunting parties who went after Indians purportedly to punish them for some perceived misdemeanour but in truth acting more like a sporting expedition) in all probability fulfilled modern-day definitions of the crime of genocide.

Henry Radcliffe's attitude towards the Native American population of California was consistent with that held by the majority of the incoming population arriving from other parts of America, from Mexico and from Europe.

The *Stockton Times* took an unusually benign and enlightened view of the Californian Indian population. In the issue of 26 March

1851 it stated: 'The Indians have been shamefully maltreated and imposed upon.' This was in straight contradiction of the view held by the *Daily Alta California* newspaper, which, in an editorial on 17 March 1851, said, 'We must now chastise these mountain thieves and murderers into submission, or annihilate them.'

It is to be assumed that the sentiments expressed in the *Stockton Times* were those of John White, as Henry was away on an expedition to the mountains during most of March 1851. Henry's personal views, however regrettable to modern ways of thinking, coincided with those of the *Daily Alta California*. He was all for striking 'the final stroke in extermination of the dark Indian race'. In a long letter of 20 January 1851 to John he says:

> **It is an unjust war – but there is no help for it – we are here: gold we must have: we cannot refrain from hunting either for sport or to fill our hungry bellies with deer meat, elk or bear. If the Indians will work we will supply food clothing and drink. If however they must have their hunting grounds – if that is necessary for them – why then John we must kill them or they will kill us for which I cannot be brought to see the reason – the wild man must go hence and be no more seen.**

Henry Radcliffe in expressing himself as he did, was just going with the flow. There were not enough voices raised in opposition to save the Indians from their inexorable fate. Indians who sought to come to terms with the Europeans found themselves consigned to reservations miles from their native lands, where they faced starvation and death. Those who resisted were systematically hunted down and killed.

When Henry arrived in San Francisco in the late summer of 1849, California had only been in American hands for some three years. Even in the months prior to July 1848 it was only de facto control. In 1846 the Americans had raised the Stars and Stripes at Monterey,[12] Yerba Buena (San Francisco), Sonoma and New Helvetia without encountering any real resistance from the Mexican authorities. The Mexicans had little option but to acquiesce. Added to this was the fact that the military commander was an advocate of Californian independence while the Governor (Pico Pico) actually suggested that California should become a British Protectorate! Mexican rule was very tenuous. There were small townships at San Jose, Santa Cruz, Los Angeles and tiny garrisons at Monterey, San Francisco, Santa Barbara and, far in the south, San Diego.

California was on the remote fringe of the Mexican empire. The Central area was difficult to access, particularly overland, and the sea journey was long and dangerous. In truth Alta California (the present State of California) was an orphan state. The Spaniards had planted numerous missions all along the coastal belt but by 1846 these were in decline, as they had been secularised in 1833 following Mexico's independence from Spain in 1821.

By 1845 there was a feeling that California was ripe for the taking. The United States, fearful of the Russians, who had established a fort north of San Francisco, and the British, who had a man-of-war anchored in Monterey Bay, made the first move.

The action taken in 1846 would of itself have been an act of war but as the Mexican–American War of 1846–8 had already broken out many miles to the south, the taking of California was simply a small part of a larger conflict. When the Mexican–American War was brought to an end by the Treaty of Guadelupe Hidalgo (proclaimed on 4 July 1848) California was formally ceded to the United States.

---

[12] The historic 40' x 70' flag that was a prominent feature of the Monterey Fourth of July Parade.

The American most closely associated with the taking of California was John Charles Fremont. He was a topographical engineer in the service of the US Army. He led a small contingent of American soldiers into California on the pretext of a mapping expedition. He had tweaked Mexican noses by raising the Stars and Stripes (briefly) at Hawks Peak (now Fremont) near Monterey (the provincial capital) in 1846 but then decided not to tempt fate and marched north. On the way he heard of what we now call the Bear Flag Revolt. This involved a handful of American settlers who, fearful that the Mexican Governor might expel all foreigners, marched on Sonoma, raised the flag of the short-lived California Republic and arrested the military Governor, the redoubtable Mariano Vallejo. Vallejo began life as a Spaniard, then became a Mexican and finally became an American, serving as a Californian Senator. He gave his name to the town, which was briefly the State capital, while Benicia, a town close to Vallejo, is named after his wife.

Fremont marched his men (all sixty-two of them) to Sonoma where he absorbed the triumphant Americans into what became the California Battalion.

One of those subsequently inducted into the Battalion was James D. Savage. Savage had travelled from Illinois, suffering debilitating hardships on the six months' journey across America. He arrived at Sutter's Fort at New Helvetia on 28 October 1846, too late for the Bear Flag Revolt but joined the California Battalion under Fremont. Savage was a classic example of a California pioneer. Born in 1817, he showed an early talent for learning languages, something that would stand him in good stead when he came to dealing with the numerous tribes of Californian Indians.

By October 1846 California had been taken by the Americans. Fremont had marched his men to Monterey where he linked forces with US Naval units who on 7 July had taken Monterey without firing a shot. The local Mexican commander simply fled. As a contemporary writer (6 October 1846) noted:

> **Came into the camp late and found Carson (i.e. Kit Carson) with an express from California, leaving intelligence that that country had surrendered without a blow, and that the American flag floated in every part.**

Although there were skirmishes in the southern part of the State in late 1846 the ultimate defeat of the Mexicans was inevitable. The Treaty of Cahuenga Pass, signed by Fremont and General Andrés Pico (Governor Pico's brother) on 13 January 1847 brought Californian hostilities to an end. For a time, Fremont was able to enjoy the fruits of his success.

In 1847 he gave his agent, Thomas Larkin, who had previously been US Consul in Monterey, $3,000 to buy land near Mision San Jose. For some reason Larkin bought 45,000 acres of dry land in the vicinity of Mariposa.

When the California Battalion was disbanded in April 1847, following the signing of the Treaty of Cahuenga Pass in January of that year, James Savage sought alternative employment. He moved south to the furthest extremities of the San Joaquin Valley where he essentially 'went native'. He settled among the Tularenos (Southern Yokut) Indians and became so integrated with them that, having learned their language, he became one of their leaders. He went so far as to marry several of the daughters of the local chief. He led the Tularenos into battle with neighbouring tribes. His fair hair hung down in ringlets, giving rise to his nickname 'The Blond King'. Things might have continued like this for years had it not been for the discovery of Californian gold.

By 1849 Savage was employing hundreds of Indians to pan for gold for him in the numerous rivers that flowed down from the Sierra Nevada to the San Joaquin. He set up trading posts, first on the Merced River (a post subsequently abandoned in the face of repeated Indian attacks) and later at Agua Fria on the Mariposa, possibly with the support of Fremont who owned land in that area. He opened another trading post on the Fresno River, near Coarse Gold Gulch. The Indians resented the encroachment of the miners. Their fragile economy was threatened. The miners killed their precious game for sport and the panning of the rivers ruined their fishing.

It could have been predicted that they would fight back and so they did. They attacked Savage's store on the Merced in May 1850. In December of that year Savage's Fresno store was attacked and three men killed. This was the last straw. There followed the short-lived but, as regards the Indians, pivotal Mariposa War (December 1850–June 1851). Let Henry (20 January 1851) take up the story:

> **Mr Chalmers has just arrived from the Fresno 90 miles from Stockton with account of a great Indian fight – Mr Southern (Manchester) came also at the same moment from an expedition which started from Moquelumne Hill (east of Stockton) both parties in my opinion have been defeated. I am sorry to learn that the Indians are guided in many instances by white men – if this so – and names are mentioned-- a cruel death will be their lot. It appears the whole range of hills are infested with Indians up in arms – feathers and war paint – several men have been killed in fair fight and many parties are missing. For three months we have been aware that Indian couriers were passing from Ranch to Ranch but could not learn their motives – a boy belonging to Savage's Indians confessed but the war had commenced. It is amusing to**

hear a description of an Indian fight. They cover their heads with feathers which stand straight up and are fastened by means of their long hair – their bodies are painted – when entering into combat they make a most dreadful noise by striking continuously the hand quickly upon the lips at the same time emitting a most hideous cry which can be heard to a considerable distance and is the most startling sound I have ever heard. It must be dreadful when large numbers are together. When two or three are pursued they make off for the hills, run to the top, grin, show their backs – and appear to make fun of you by gestures and expressions, if the pursuers ascend the hill the Indians discharge their arrows squatting on the ground behind rocks or trees. When the place, from the approach of the enemy, becomes too dangerous they decamp running down the opposite side of the hill and run up the next where they again commence to mock and irritate so as to induce the pursuit to be continued. Many small parties have been cut off in this way being surprised by an ambuscade.

The Indians are dangerous enemies when they attack at night as they creep to the camp and discharge their arrows in perfect showers. In a camp which had been burnt and sacked by the Indians at the Fresno (ash) eight miles from the Aqua Frio (cold water) Chalmers assisted at the burial of three men – one of the unfortunate fellows had 22 arrows in his body – In the last fight as yet of which we have heard six white men and 26 indians have been killed the number of whites engaged were 50 and 10 of these guarded the provisions – The Indians amounted to 300 or 400 able warriors – After the battle the chief told Savage that he was ashamed his men had fought so badly but that he would have made a much better fight if his best warriors had not gone to sack Mariposa (butterfly). In a battle like this the Indians have three chiefs – one who stands out of harms way and two fighting chiefs – The non-fighting chief directs every movement and in many instances can be heard by their opponents so that it is highly necessary to have a man like Savage who has been nearly all his life among them. Savage is a very fine fellow one of natures gods well informed, he was a terror to the Californians prior to the coming of the Americans – his wives are very numerous and the tribe which he commanded numbered from 200 to 500 I never learned his history he has often said he preferred the wild life to the confined state of existence of what you term civilisation. The Indians have all left him and taken his children some of his wives refused to leave the Ranch but dared not betray their tribe to Savage. In this pursuit of the tribe after their departure so hot was it carried on that the poor squaws lightened their burden of acorns bread and meat by casting them on the ground thus affording a trail which could be easily followed during the night. – When the whites came up to a place that the Indians had just left they found one of the squaws dying from exhaustion, the poor creature had carried one of Savage's children in addition to her burden – the boy was lying upon the woman's breast almost perished with cold – Savage went out to scout he was spoken to by an Indian who told him to stand and approach no further – Go home Savage we wish you no harm – why follow the Indian Our chiefs are mighty our warriors like the waters of the rivers – they are here and will kill every American – Come not near – Savage continued to approach and called to the Indian to come near that they might talk – but the Indian pointed to a mountain a short distance from there – and said see Savage our warriors are approaching. Savage made a hasty retreat and told the company that upwards of 600 Indians were closing upon them – the company were 15 in number and although so few could hardly be persuaded to fly. An American believes he is a match for everything when armed with his Colt and rifle and so they are – nearly so – as each man may be counted as six before he commences to reload his weapons. The Indians are as cunning [as] they are and never or very seldom exposes his body it is the same with the Americans every one fights upon his own hook and places himself behind a tree and fires when he is certain and never wastes a ball. – Savage's opinion is that nothing but driving the Indian far into the snowy mountains will do and that it must be done immediately for in summer we cannot fight them for the foliage and the abundance of food – This John simply means if the Indian will run and not be shot why he must starve or be frozen and so the race exterminated.

The Mariposa War lasted a brief six months. By June 1851 the Indians had been forced to accept reservation status. One of the unexpected dividends of the campaign was the discovery (at least by Europeans) of the Yosemite Valley in March 1851. It was an unequal conflict. The Americans could call upon military assistance from the Californian Governor. In fact, 200 regular soldiers were sent from San Francisco to help with the subjugation of the Indians. The ubiquitous Judge Marvin left his post at the *Sonora Herald* to become Commissary and Quarter Master of the California Mounted Volunteers, based at Stockton.

Marvin was a witness to the murder of James Savage in August

1852. Details of his killing vary but it seems he protested at the senseless killing of Indians on the reservation at the Kings River, to the south. His adversary, Walter Harvey, was the culprit and Savage challenged him. In the ensuing fight Harvey managed to lay hands on a revolver, whether his or Savage's is not clear, and shot Savage four times. Savage was only thirty-four when he died. 'His Indians' were inconsolable.

CHAPTER 5
Hopes and Disappointments

In April 1850 Henry wrote to John that his heart was sad on account of having been

> deceived in an individual who had charge of my trading tent at the Mariposa and who has let me down $2000 in gold dust – it is hard to lose what you have fixed in your mind on for three months to gain nothing but fame after having led the way to relieve your fellow man – up a rapid river in the depth of winter continually rowing for 21 days exposed to rain and cold in an open boat and then having accomplished your object – the undertaking being in the first instance induced from a shade of humanity as well as a desire of gain at the risk of your life to lose what has absolutely been received over and above your first costs – God forgive me but I am sorrowful who ought to be exceedingly glad.

On the other hand, in the very same letter Henry says:

> I would I could send you a part of my dreadful healthy health, I cannot reduce myself, the most violent riding long continued only throws me into a profuse perspiration and I grow stouter and stouter – my mind is entirely changed my views of life, the manner in which it should be spent and enjoyed – wholly different – I cannot conceive any country so great as California for grand excitement. What are parties – balls – dinners etc to our money making

Part of Main Road, Ballarat 1859. Francis Cogne (Rex Nan Kivell Collection, National Library of Australia).

Diggers at Eagle Hawk Gully, Bendigo. GF Angas (La Trobe Collection, State Library of Victoria).

En route to the Diggings. William Strutt (Victoria Parliament Library).

Fryers Creek, Mount Alexander Diggings [a view], 1850-1859 S.T. Gill (Dixson Library, State Library of New South Wales).

Fair Prospects. S.T. Gill (National Library of Australia).

Cradling, Forest Creek 1852, 1850-1859 S.T. Gill (Dixson Library, State Library of New South Wales).

Gold Washing at the Ballarat Diggings 1851. William Strutt (Victoria Parliament Library).

The New Rush (1864). S.T Gill. (National Gallery of Victoria, Melbourne).

Gold Mining. Edward Roper (Rex Nan Kivell Collection/Wiki).

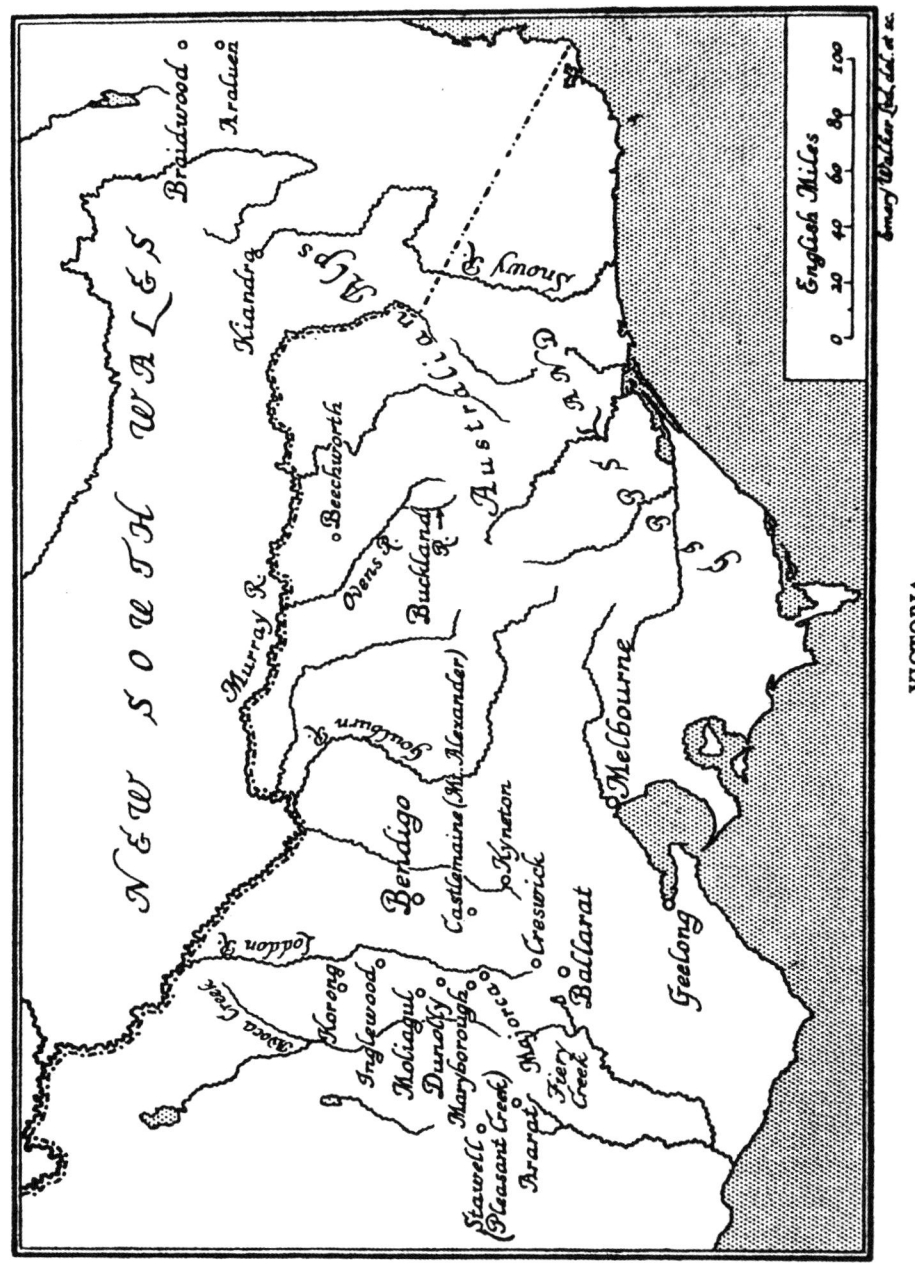

Map of Victoria. Emery Walker. (Wiki).

Back Creek Bendigo looking towards Epsom 1860 John Thomas Doyle & Samuel Thomas Gill (Mitchell Library, State Library of New South Wales).

Ballarat Gold Fields. S.T. Gill (Wiki).

Ballarat, 1853. Eugene von Guerard (Wiki).

Pegleg Gully near Ballarat 1854. Australasian Sketcher. (Victoria State Govt).

Looking south along Sturt Street from the Southern Cross Hotel to the Town Hall tower in background, Ballarat c1870. (Mitchell Library, State Library of New South Wales).

Ballarat District Hospital c1870 (Mitchell Library, State Library of New South Wales).

amusements – hardships we endure but I do not speak of them because you could not understand them and why men rush into them and call them the height of enjoyment.

Generally, Henry exudes confidence. On 30 August 1850 he writes to John: 'You must not fear for me for I am perfectly comfortable and happy except a little irritation occasionally – no place like California for making a man subdue his passions and to teach him to be cool and determined.' The final sentence of that letter reads: 'Do not despair I shall in all human probability get rich and come home to see you all.'

In a letter to Kate dated 14 May 1851 Henry says, 'Now do not be anxious on my account I am in fine spirits and except for a few sores on the lips and ears usually left after an attack of fever I am a stronger and better man than when I left Knotty Ash.' Adding, 'I shall soon find my way up although as I write I am all but cleaned out.' However, he adds a few lines later, 'I only write to prevent you and my brother becoming anxious on my account and to assure you and them that I feel in better spirits than I have enjoyed for the last three months and that the determination to overcome all difficulties is greater than ever.'

Henry tells John:

> We have been presented with six lots in Tuolumne City, three in Crescent City and I am requested to go and select from Sonora Grace Town and the French Camp – Weber of Stockton offered us only <u>one lot</u>[13] for doing what no man could or would do for his own Town – the offer was too small to enter into our consideration – this man has not performed his promise and we are glad of it for it renders our paper independent.

---

[13] Underlining in the original.

He must have owned a bit of property because elsewhere he says:

The seat of government is very likely to be removed from San Jose to Vallejo where we have 16 lots if this finally takes place I shall be perfectly contented with my luck in California.

In a postscript to his letter to John of 20 January 1851 he says: 'Vallejo has passed the Senate only one opposing vote Land must go up – bad and good news.'

Henry's hopes of a killing in Vallejo came to nothing, however. The State legislature (California having been granted Statehood by President Millard Fillmore on 9 September 1850) met originally in San Jose, midway between San Francisco and the old Mexican capital of Monterey. The delegates hated the little town. It had none of the modest creature comforts they were used to. Thus, it was that the vote was cast to move to Vallejo much to the delight of Mariano Vallejo, one time Spaniard who became a Mexican general, now a California Senator. His delight (and Henry's, for that matter) was, however, short lived. After a degree of shuttling between Vallejo, Sacramento and Benicia (which served as State capital for more than a year), Sacramento finally secured the honour of being State capital in February 1854. Henry never reports what happened to the 16 lots in Vallejo. Despite his protestations Henry was having a tough time in Stockton. A hint of all not being well comes at the end of his letter to Kate of 14 May 1851: 'Tell John I will write a long letter to him when I begin to look up.'

He was endlessly striving to allay concerns felt by his family. In his letter to Kate of 30 June 1851 he says:

Dear Kate I am more anxious concerning you and John's

feeling sorry for me than anything that has happened and I must again assure you that I am really happy – now listen I eat well, drink of the best and except two nights last Monday and Tuesday sleep well – faith the love of money could not purchase a bed for thousands or even a covering but what was that to me no great hardship when I have laid for weeks out for pleasure – further I am not anxious for the future, money in different quantities comes regularly – indeed except the ordinary troubles of life and they to me are very few I may say I am completely happy – God be thanked.

Ever the optimist he adds:

I have averaged $8 per day, a small sum I grant and only a little more than my expenses but expect as soon as my plans are carried out to equal my best days in California.

The year 1851 was the one of the Great Exhibition at the Crystal Palace in London. Henry's friend Arrowsmith, who returned to England carrying letters and gold for the Radcliffes in Liverpool, delayed his arrival in order to visit the exhibition. In her letter of 3 July 1851 (returned to sender) Kate says:

Richard (Henry's brother) and his wife have been to the Exhibition. We do not intend to go and instead of going John has bought me a Brougham and the horse we had before you left England is to run in it, it is coming home tomorrow.

Writing to John on 29 February 1851 Henry says:

My dear John,

A large number of Californians have left for the world fair. I am afraid their habits will not suit the English although of all men I fancy they will conduct themselves the most orderly yet I am certain they will never be able to bear any restraint which would appear to them as an insult which from habit they will resent. I fear they will carry their arms which they could hardly be persuaded to lay aside and this is not to be wondered at as many are from Texas and the frontiers and have never from 12 years of age been without the rifle, pistol or knife.

I sincerely trust they will meet with due consideration and will be well received for of all Americans I admire them the most. When you become acquainted with them you'll find covered by their roughness more fine honourable feeling than falls to the lot of most men. They resemble in many traits of character the idea in form of the old English knight – abjectly devoted to the fair sex, naturally courteous brave and rash. There is a marked difference between the Southern men and Yankee (northern) indeed you may always distinguish them and I prefer the South notwithstanding the slaves. I persuade as far as I can everyone I meet not to go to England but they say they want to see the fair and learn if there is no bragging in the matter. Should you ever meet one of the 'hombres' remember everything is new to him you will find he is acquainted with history to some extent and as read of form customs etc, but you are not to forget that the whole of life has been passed in the forests and mountains – that he knows nothing of cities and their amusements. All Americans speak freely this is to be attributed to their national education of independence and it is a great advantage over our own countrymen few of whom can speak before a dozen strangers.

He clearly had very warm feelings for his family back in Liverpool. His concern for his brothers and sister is apparent. Indeed George, to whom he wrote just before leaving Liverpool, was constantly in his thoughts. In his letter to John of 20 January 1851 he writes, 'I regret exceedingly to learn from Kate of my mother's want of due attention and of the continued misconduct of the boy George.' Kate wrote to him on 3 July 1851 (*a letter that he never received*), 'I wish we could say so (*ie. that he was good and steady*) of that fellow George he gets worse instead of better and will not do anything in the shape of work if he has clothes given to him he pawns them John gave him a very handsome jacket which he pawned for 2 shillings John is the only one who gives him anything and allows him 8d a week I think he should not give him any and then when left entirely without he would perhaps do something for himself.' Later that year John wrote (*again not received by Henry*), 'George I do not know anything of him. I allow him 3/– per week and Reg-d (*Reginald, another brother*) allows him 2/–.' Just over a year later poor George was admitted to Crichton Royal Hospital near Dumfries in Scotland, one of the earliest private mental hospitals. He would remain institutionalised for the rest of his life. His brothers in Liverpool would have covered the expense.

Henry would worry over what was to happen to his sister Maryanne when their mother died. On 30 June 1851 he writes to Kate, 'I am sorry for Maryanne her condition must be very lonely if my former state existed now I would offer her a comfortable berth in the Hospital and give her a parlour in addition.' He is endlessly solicitous about his nephews Tom, Ned and Harry. He could not resist issuing advice on how they should be brought up. He clearly missed the family circle.

Henry struggled in the latter half of 1851. The fire in Stockton in May left him 'all but cleaned out'. He describes how, two nights after reaching Stockton on 4 May, 'that unfortunate City was fired by some demon and in two hours our beautiful Town, and to me dearly loved, was gone yes hardly a piece of charred wood left so completely had the fire done its work'. He adds, 'I turned out with the rest, we all did our best but to no purpose.'

He estimated the loss of property in Stockton at more than $1,000,000. There was a fire at the same time in San Francisco. Henry comments, 'San Francisco has not been nearly as completely destroyed as Stockton although the damage of course is ten times as great.'

By June 1851 Henry had left Stockton and returned to San Francisco. His losses in Stockton were compounded by a second fire, which raged in San Francisco on 22 June, just after he had set up his small doctor's store in Kearney Street. Despite all the adversity he continued to exude optimism.

However, when news came of the discovery of gold in Australia, he appears to have tried to 'disappear'. Perhaps he thought of himself as a failure; perhaps he had racked up debts and thought the easiest way to evade his creditors was to run away.

Sometime in 1852 Henry embarks for Sydney and there is what appears to be seven and a half years of silence. His last letter from California is short:

San Francisco Dec 12th 1851

My dear John,

> The bearer is a young gentleman who I have known for some time in Stockton and in this town. He is returning home from California via Liverpool and as I am perfectly

> aware it will be a source of gratification to converse with him I have given him an introduction so extend your welcome to him and oblige your
>
> Affect. Brother
>
> PS Love to all at home

It must have been very worrying for the family in Liverpool when Kate's and John's letters were returned as 'uncollected'.

Given that Henry established the first newspaper in Stockton as well as the first hospital and was involved in the founding of the first church, quite apart from leading various prospecting expeditions to the wilds, he must surely be considered one of the founding fathers of the City of Stockton, on a par with Weber, who is generally accredited with being *the* founding father of Stockton.

CHAPTER 6
Australia

John and Kate back in Liverpool found that their letters (3 July and their joint letter dated 24 October and 6 November 1851 sent to Stockton) were never collected. Henry had told them on 14 May to address their letters to him care of the San Francisco post office, but Kate had already posted her letter by the time Henry's letter arrived in Liverpool. Why the letter of 24 October/6 November was not collected or forwarded is a mystery. Most likely Henry left for Australia in the early days of 1852 before the letter arrived.

The return of the uncollected letters must have caused considerable anxiety in Liverpool. It would be a good five years before Henry's presence in Australia became known. We know that Kate wrote to him in Australia on 10 November 1857, but that letter did not reach him for another two years. Correspondence between the brothers restarted in 1859 when, on 13 June, Henry wrote from Back Creek, Amherst, in the State of Victoria:

> My dear John,
>
> I have just received your letter dated 19th January I will not attempt to express the warm gush of feeling it occasioned.
>
> My heart like yours beats with the same young blood as in the days long long passed away. It was my desire and wish that you and all that I fondly cherished might never have heard of me – fate has determined otherwise

and as I have never, through my varied life, shrunk from what I have thought at the time to be my duty – so now – however painful, I must again commune with those from whom my heart has never been separated.

You and I, John, will rejoice that Harry has never disgraced the good old name – Radcliffe – true he has filled many grades of life – he has worked till the blood has oozed from his fingers – he has hunted for an existence – he has been a determined gold digger – a store keeper and what not – but he has asked no favours or received any. Sometimes he has been on a fair road to fortune, at least independence and then --------- begins the world de novo – Such has been my history. Now I have become indifferent to fortune, it never troubles me – I thank God for the blessings I do enjoy and have enjoyed. I am contented – cheerful and at times very happy – my wants are few and may be comprised in a canvas roof – tobacco – dogs – horse & time – So much for Harry – he must not come back – he is rough unmannerly and not too accommodating – Our lives have been opposite, yet we must have much in common, the warm love of country – Old England – The heart aching after home – the dread of ill to those we love & let us trust our God – worshipped by one, beneath a gilded roof, by the other in the wild dreamy wood – May He in his extreme goodness have mercy on both & should it not be that we meet in this life, may He grant that we receive His blessing in a reunion hereafter. I ask not for Kate. I know her loving heart – her pleasant smile is upon me as I write. Would that I had never caused it for a moment to fade – her children – how bright and joyous – the picture has too warm a glow of sunshine – far too bright for me to dwell upon without the anguish of repining.

Dearest John – Kate brothers and all receive my grateful thanks, more I have not, for your long love and above all, rest assured, that he who has caused you much anxiety, fears not his fate – he believes his destiny is realised – he knows that his life has been a total failure & although he values little what most cling to – yet he will not shrink but endure with God's assistance to the end. Good bye

H.H. Radcliffe

Quite why Henry wished to cut himself off from the family he loved so dearly is not obvious. In his next letter to John (14 July 1859) he writes: 'Upon receipt of your letter dated 16th April I wrote to Messrs Bright Bros. to return the money you generously sent. It was to avoid being a burden to you and my brothers that I have so long abstained from writing.' Perhaps the answer lies in the words in his previous letter: 'he knows that his life has been a total failure'. But he was only forty and in due course his fortunes improved.

Serious quantities of gold were not found in Australia until 1851. The first meaningful discovery was in New South Wales where there was a major rush. But this was a mere prologue to the Victorian gold rush. An offer of a reward of 200 guineas for the discovery of a profitable goldfield within 200 miles of Melbourne produced a result. In August 1851, gold in significant quantities was found near Ballarat. Thus, the Victorian gold rush began. By the end of October that year, 6,000 to 7,000 hopeful diggers had made their way to Ballarat and to other nearby areas where finds had been made. Men poured in, mostly from Melbourne,

Tasmania and South Australia with some from New South Wales.

The news of the Australian gold discoveries reached London in November 1851. By June 1852 an army of gold-hungry immigrants had begun to arrive in Melbourne. As the rush got under way people flooded into Victoria. The modest New South Wales rush was dwarfed. Some 94,000 hopefuls arrived in Victoria in 1852, many from California bringing their skills and equipment with them. As Henry started out early from San Francisco on hearing of the New South Wales gold discoveries he would probably have landed in Sydney and made for the Bathurst area, perhaps Ophir or the Turon River, where the initial discoveries were made. He could have got wind of the Australian finds earlier than most Europeans, which may explain his presumed departure from San Francisco early in 1852. Let Henry take up the story (his letter to John of 14 July 1859 in response to understandable requests to tell his family what he had been up to):

> **I entered the colony with 2/6 in my pocket** *[equivalent to 12½p in modern money]* **walked in patent leather boots 120 miles arrived at the diggings with 2/6. Dug got £200 came to Sydney tried to get into practice as a surgeon** *[clearly his earlier distaste for medical practice had abated]* **lost my last 50 pounds either from my pocket or from my bedroom – cut wood became a crack bushman – bought a horse started on a journey to the Ovens 400 miles on 28/–** [£1.40 *in today's money*].

The first Ovens River rush was in October 1852; it was one of the earliest Victorian rushes, attracting thousands from the worked-out alluvial deposits at Ballarat. The Ovens River, north of the Australian Alps, on the border with New South Wales and about 140 miles from Melbourne, offered the advantage of copious water for panning and washing the 'pay dirt'. It was, however, remote, and in winter there were doubts about getting supplies. By New Year 1853 there were nearly 20,000 diggers there. But it was short lived, and the number of diggers quickly declined, especially after hearing of further major finds at Ballarat.

It is impossible to pinpoint exactly when Henry went to the Ovens River as there was a new rush in January 1854 involving 5,000 to 6,000 miners. He may have been one of them. Henry goes on: 'Made money at the Ovens invested in horses with Peters a Welshman went to Melbourne lost by the [*illegible*] left for Forest Creek.'

The passing reference to 'Peters' raises the intriguing question of whether this Peters could have been the same Peters who made the important gold discovery on a sheep-run within a few miles of Mount Alexander, seventy miles north-west of Melbourne. Mount Alexander turned out to be one of the richest areas. By the middle of December 1851 many of the diggers who had rushed to Ballarat moved on to Mount Alexander. By December there were 20,000 at the new discoveries and only 300 left at Ballarat. If nothing else this illustrates the immense ebb and flow of diggers from one rush to another.

The rush to Forest Creek (in the Mount Alexander prospecting district, renamed Castlemaine in 1854) was one of the most profitable of all the early rushes. It started in the late summer of 1852 (that is, in March and April of that year). In those days, Forest Creek did not really live up to its name. A *Melbourne Argus*' correspondent wrote:

> The road, which winds along the creek through the diggings, is, from the constant traffic, ten times more dusty than even dusty Melbourne, and the heavy gusts of wind, which pour through the gullies with great violence,

whirl it up in clouds, and scatter it far and near upon everything around. The newly-erected tent does not, therefore, retain its brilliant whiteness. … In the same way, such trees as have escaped the axe are dusted to an unnatural brownness. … Even off the road, the earth is so trodden and worn by the thousands of feet that are constantly passing and repassing, that not the faintest sign of verdure remains upon the ground … while, on the southern side of the creek, the hills are so pierced, and the subsoil so tossed and tumbled about upon their face, that they look like nothing but gravel or chalk-pits and stone-quarries. When to this is also added the constant feeding of the innumerable horses which throng the diggings, eating off the grass on the few hills that have not been ransacked, and even cropping the shoots of the few shrubs that grow amongst the rocks, baring them of every particle of verdure, and the rude, rough look of the jagged rocks which protrude from the bare surface – anything but a refreshing picture meets the eye.

At Forest Creek, Henry 'fell in with one of Aiken's sons – a bad one, the most ungrateful dog I have ever met he stole my horse saddle etc sold them & I forgave him for the sake of old Liverpool'.

He says he became a government contractor and made money. Then he joined the rush to Jones' Creek. This rush at a creek four miles north of the Victorian town of Dunolly took place in June 1856. It did not last long; Henry found himself 'left alone' and 'obliged to hook it also'. He then prospected for nine months and found gold but 'had no protection'.

He returned to the Mount Alexander area, to Campbell's Creek, which he describes as 'done up' (maybe he was describing himself). His letter goes on: 'preached a sermon beneath an old gum tree raised 30/– found an old hole earned £9 per week for six months – struck gold upon a Hill (Doctor's Hill) got a share of £1000 became a storekeeper thought it demeaning to stand behind a counter so of course I was soon done brown [*he must mean 'down'*] – left to Mount Ararat.'

The Mount Ararat (present day Ararat) rush began in late 1857, then Australian summer. Henry's move to Mount Ararat allows us to fix more accurately his movements while he was out of communication with his family.

By June 1859 his address was Back Creek, Amherst. There was a rush there early in 1859. Henry lived in Scandinavian Crescent, the main street of Back Creek, until he moved on to Inglewood in March 1860 to try his luck at yet another rush. He mentions to John: 'I have a grand house – wooden floor which you must admit is coming it strong towards civilisation.' Back Creek is today known as Talbot. It is 32 miles north of Ballarat. Nearby are the vestiges of the town of Amherst (formerly known as Daisy Hill Creek).

Henry's description of the twelve months or so between Mount Ararat and Back Creek are easier to decipher. He seems to have got into a little trouble at Mount Ararat – where he 'found gold a rich hill rushed by Chinamen – a battle a few broken heads – burnt Chinamen's tents bloodshed up before the magistrates'. There were thousands of Chinese participating in the Victorian gold rush. They began to arrive after 1854, and by 1858 they numbered 33,000. They suffered from bigotry and racism especially at the Buckland River diggings (near the Ovens River) and Mount Ararat where they were expelled and, as Henry witnesses, their tents burned.

After Mount Ararat, Henry went back to Dunolly where he

worked the Horses £27 per week thought of Home & dear old England fancied myself walking in Liverpool

with my red shirt etc, rush over – one more trial and then good-bye – quartz claim next to one from which 52oz of gold was taken from a bucketful of surface stone – lost or stolen from the drays three horses at £85 £120 and £130 could blame no-one – hunted for them five months – Quartz reef a duffer down to 111ft, gave up (this hole was 6 months afterwards sunk four or six feet and is now working as rich as the first claim). Went to wet sinking erected machinery got into working order – fell down a hole next to my own tent – inflammation of knee – used up – in despair turned Doctor.

It is almost certain that he is describing events that happened in September 1858. After three weeks confined to his tent and, as he put it, 'minus the needful', Henry agreed to take charge of a druggist store at the Havelock diggings 'for rest was necessary'. Gold had been found there in 1858. Havelock was ten miles north of Maryborough on the road to Dunolly. Henry writes, 'During the twelve weeks I was thus engaged the business steadily increased and although I received no pay, except food, I was induced to remain for the sake of gaining a name.' He moved on to Clunes, twenty-two miles north of Ballarat, where gold had been discovered as early as 1851. He remained there until early March 1859, only clearing his expenses. He then moved on to Back Creek and the resumption of correspondence with his brother.

CHAPTER 7
Doctor or Drugstore

The relief felt by Henry's family in Liverpool when they heard that he was still alive must have been enormous. They responded in the only way they could, sending him money, which Henry, ever proud and reluctant to depend on his brothers, sent back. As his business experiences running the druggist store in Havelock had persuaded him that such activities would provide a rather better standard of living than the one he had endured in the goldfields, on 14 July 1859 he wrote to John, 'I left the Clunes for my present residence and entered into an arrangement with Mr Page druggist for board and half fees – A man without money must be contented with very little – Moreover I have had to contend against the opposition of nearly all the profession here, who denounced me as unqualified and a quack this is annoying but I trust will soon be obviated.'

Henry then details the fees he has taken as a doctor over the period 7 March to 11 July. They average £12–11–5 per week (about £12.62 in present-day money). He compares this with the takings of a druggist.

> The money taken in the shop exclusive of fees has averaged £50 per week, giving, allowing for loss etc., a profit of £40 per week out of which we must deduct my board and Page's personal expenses. We have debts amounting to £100 most of which if looked after would be paid, indeed they may be considered as good as all doubtful cases are not booked: The rush is dying away the main lead having been worked into wet sinking and the body of miners

leaving I shall again only be able to earn a bare living at best Drugs etc are very dear in Melbourne and although I might obtain credit yet I must pay cent per cent for it. My object is to follow the rushes till fortune gives me a good opening on a new field when a township will be formed and there remain. To be purely a doctor is out of the question as you will perceive from the above statement the profit of the druggist is tenfold. I have saved £80 during the eight months having had a horse and clothes to buy If I had had a shop during the same period I might have wrote £1000 – All depends so much on chance in this country that I am truly disgusted with money hunting thus I might move to a place which as far as I could learn was to turn out well – and one month afterwards be left alone without having cleared my expenses. Should you from this description of my position dare to advance me in drugs & the sum of £50 consigned to Bright Bro I will do my utmost to repay the same as well as our former account. I enclose a list of articles from which a wholesale house must select to make the amount. My old friend, Charles Higgins who I understand is in business would be a proper person and might prove desirous to serve me – Understand that I have no confidence in my luck for I am so accustomed to reverses that a continuance of prosperity is the exception and it would not astonish me to wake tomorrow with the little I have burning around me. I have thought at times that surely I must be cursed for I have sought peace and have not found it. I have endured hardship without a murmur. My sorrow I have kept to myself.

Henry seems not to appreciate the inconsistency between sending back John's and Reginald's money and asking them to forward drugs and £50. He must have worried them even more when he wrote in the same letter:

> So John from this outline you may form an idea of your brother Harry – is it possible that he can get on – in truth I don't credit it – if he had a shop it would certainly be burnt or destroyed for everything he has ever tried ended suddenly and went to pot.
>
> I would gladly write to Kate and did intend to do so but feel so depressed after recalling my past life that I have not the heart to carry out my wish.

By August he had picked himself up and was focusing on getting himself recognised as a surgeon or doctor.

August 12th
1859 Back Creek

My dear Brother,

I sent a copy of a letter received by this mail from the College of Surgeons refusing to furnish me with a certificate of having obtained their diploma. I sent the affidavit through Mr. Hughes of Melbourne who employed his agent in London. I trust this last party will communicate with you. I have supplied him with the necessary funds. I cannot give any further evidence of the loss of the diploma than that contained in the affidavit nor can I conceive what more they want. I have not time to make another affidavit indeed barely time to write – I shall have to leave business and take to the bush until I can become recognised here for I cannot bear to be looked down upon. I have directed Messrs. Bright Broth & Co. to return the £20 sent by Regy this mail.

Surely if my case is properly represented to the College they would not be so unjust as to refuse me – I shall send an affidavit of my loss of the Ap. Hall Diploma next mail either will answer my purpose but one I must and will have should I have to come to England for it.

I think it advisable to write to the College this mail and I hope I shall be able to make some impression upon them. With dearest love to Kate and the little ones believe me

Your affect. brother

H.H. RADCLIFFE
To John Radcliffe Esq.

There was clearly a demand for doctors and Henry was wholly justified in seeking to have his qualifications recognised in Victoria. In 'A lady's visit to the gold diggings in Australia in 1852–53' the author, Ellen Clacy, sets the scene in Forest Creek (now Castlemaine):

> It is no joke to get ill on the diggings; doctors make you pay for it. Their fees are – for a consultation, at their own tent, ten shillings; for a visit out from one to ten pounds… Many are regular quacks, and these seem to flourish best. The principal illnesses are weakness of sight, from the hot winds and sandy soil, and dysentery…. often caused by badly-cooked food, bad water, and want of vegetables.

John had been busy in Liverpool preparing an affidavit (it was dated 14 October 1859) in support of Henry's struggle to be recognised. It is doubtful if this was ever used since in a letter to Kate dated 11 October 1859 he says:

> I visited Melbourne and became a member of the Medical Board it cost me £50 to collect the evidence and prove my identity. I was occupied three weeks as I travelled over 500 miles I fortunately established everything from my hospital practice in Liverpool – voyage in the Ajax sojourn in California – my life in Australia to the present moment.

Henry was just in time. Compulsory registration of legally qualified practitioners came into force in Victoria in 1862. The first list of practitioners after the 1862 Act contained 712 names. By 1869 Henry would be an established Ballarat doctor but in the meantime his restlessness persisted and the mirage of untold wealth in the goldfields still drew him on. Ever prone to believe he could ride two horses at the same time (publishing and prospecting in California) his ambition was to run his own druggist-cum-doctors business while at the same time looking for gold. At his request John and Reginald sent him several cargos of drugs from England. In a letter dated 16 January 1860 Henry writes:

> My dear John,
>
> I have received your letter and bill of lading of goods per William Carvill and am anxiously looking for her arrival. We have another of those immense rushes taking place 12 miles from this place [*possibly Lamplough*] but I have

not moved. I would have done so had the drugs arrived in time. The Back Creek is reduced to one in twenty of its former busy occupants [*further evidence of the mass movement of miners in search of gold*] and my business is fast drawing to a very low ebb. The prospects are bright at present there being good indications of new country now prospecting being opened for which I shall be in time. I shall use every caution and return the money as taken monthly.

In the same letter Henry makes an interesting, if sad, passing comment: 'Poor Mrs Rose returned to England in the Royal Charter and I see her name has [sic] lost.'

The Royal Charter was the luxurious clipper ship, wrecked off Anglesey on its way to Liverpool with huge loss of life (and gold) during the summer of 1859.

Henry worries endlessly about his financial situation. He says, 'I do not complain but it cannot stand at a pound a day when I shall have to "hook it" and take a claim elsewhere.' He rounds off this letter in typical style: 'From my letter you will gather my mode of life it may be summed up as follows – smoking – tea drinking 2 galls daily or thereabouts – reading hunting and doctoring.'

By March 1860 the drugs had arrived safely in Back Creek. But Henry reports that Back Creek was 'all but done up' as there had been two large rushes, one at Lamplough about 10 miles from Back Creek and another that was extremely promising at Inglewood 50 miles in the interior. He writes on 15 March: 'I leave for Englewood [sic] next week all my ready cash will be required for moving etc. but afterwards I shall remit monthly. With an ordinary share of luck I shall clear the drugs in a few months.'

In another interesting aside Henry says, 'A very fine wine has been produced in Sydney equal to anything for our climate that I have ever tasted – light – acid and yet with a body – we shall soon drink wine as water.' Henry would have done well in advertising.

Henry still clings to the idea of being a doctor. He writes: 'They told me last summer that the doctor would have plenty of work for 12 months and this has come true for we have had a fearful amount of sickness and a greater number of deaths than have ever occurred before.' Another throwaway line is worth recording: 'Our people are becoming too levelling in their political ideas and instead of liberty we shall soon equal America in despotism.'

One wonders what Henry's views were on the Eureka Stockade (Eureka Rebellion) (1854). Did he perhaps participate? Sadly, this was during the period when he was out of contact with his family.

Henry's views on his adopted country contain echoes of his earlier views on San Francisco. Writing to John on 16 January 1860 he says:

> The climate is not healthy and ten years residence adds ten to most mens ages [*as it would!*] – it is hard to rear children and women are like cracked parchment at 20 to 25. So much for Australia, the happy – its animals were made in the year 1 its rivers gutters, its forests clothed in rags without song in its birds or odour in its flowers – who would change it for healthy clouded old England with its bursts of sunshine – cold clear water – and the inimitable colours of its ever changing foliage.

Clearly after more than ten years away from England Henry had a bad case of nostalgia that encouraged a somewhat jaundiced view of his new home.

His view had not changed by March when he told John, 'For there can be no doubt that the climate of Australia is exceedingly depressing and hurrys on age too soon. I am much older than you in appearance.' Perhaps one should note here that Henry outlived all his siblings, dying at Ballarat at the age of eighty-three.

Henry still has fond memories of his sister-in-law Kate. Of the eight letters we have between June 1859 and November 1860 (there was only one other, a rather rambling tale written to his nephew Harry in 1868) there is only one to Kate, dated 11 October 1859:

> Australia
> Scandinavian Crescent
> Back Creek

My dear Kate,
I have just received your letter dated Nov. 10th 1857 through a friend who fell in with James Dowdall in Melbourne who deserves my warmest thanks for his kindness in keeping my letters so long and I have wrote to him giving him every praise.

You ask for my likeness I would send it this mail but unfortunately my lady Tilly has become so stout that her figure is not elegant and I desire her to be in prime order so as really to make a picture not that you have not beauties in England fairer than her but she is all to me faithful kind and affectionate – her head is resting on my knee and her large eyes are watching my hand as I write – then her courage is dauntless and her knowledge very great. Her former husband Major was killed at the claims by a kangaroo which weighed 194 lbs and measured 10 ft. from the tip of the tail to the ear. We carried Tilly who was severely injured five miles and I nursed her for two weeks before her ladyship could raise herself and walk. Her present mate is a lordly fellow weight 84 lbs in hunting condition as yet has not distinguished himself being only 20 months old if I except his propensities for thieving which are truly awful nothing is too high too great or too small, from a tin of butter or an egg to half a shop all are brought daily home – he is called Doctor by the diggers – in faith he must alter his manners for he is become too savage – the other day he entered a tent and took a digger's dinner from the table turning the poor wife out. I must give him some wholesome correction although it will be much against my will – I intend sending if possible my two dogs, a kangaroo and my humble self, provided you do the same with regard to yourself and the dear little ones. I am not altered in the least except my face which a few months ago was the colour of your dinner table with the skin coming off the nose lips and cheek bones, but now being less exposed I am becoming more civilised looking but not by any means passable for your drawing room – My digging weight averaged 12 st. to which I have added 9 lbs of flabby fat anything but an agreeable addition in this climate – I regret to learn from your letter of so many deaths of those whom I left gay and young – the reverse is however satisfactory, for the command 'go forth and multiply' seems to have been strictly obeyed and even those who have not entirely fulfilled the order have taken the necessary steps – who would have thought that the staid prim Emma Lindley (qv.) or the fastidious Mary Platt would have had the courage to enter into the dread bonds of wedlock. It is a strange world – all chance – a puff of wind – an ill spoken word – a glance – a gesture – make or mar a man. I who from boyhood have longed to possess a wife – to prize cherish and love with my whole soul am now beyond all hope with a dog for my companion.

You ask for a history of my life, Kate it may be summed in a few words – a life of toil and what you in England would term hardships and privations indeed when I look back I wonder how it is that I am still here and have passed through it with a cheerful spirit and a thankful heart. But away with the past and its gloom – time the future has no bright sunshine for me. I must do my duty. I trust its offices are useful. Sternly – contentedly and thankfully. How much greater is your mission to cherish to watch to support to glory in your offspring, may it be ordained that they return your love a thousandfold and when the time comes that the almond tree blossoms may their hands protect and their voices murmur sweet music of love and gentle peace.

There are many in England that I have dearly loved and still love – to me, the naughty Jane Johnson – she must be a good wife, for she was all goodness – this is the first time I have ever wrote or mentioned her name since my return from London to Liverpool in the year 43 or 44 and then sweet Jenny Jenkins she was a little love – but beyond all my dearly loved – much wronged Miss Martin – God bless her – she was a woman fitted to mate with the greatest – how glorious must she have been in the freshness of her beauty – I never saw a face as I so much admired or heard a voice that pleased me more – and many others you do not know.

And now Kate I must bid you good bye, we shall not meet on earth – but I believe in an after life – can we not be joined there – can we not then understand the various impulses of the heart which have made and controlled our actions. We shall then see clearly what is now dark and doubtful. I have recently lost a friend a few words in a hurried conversation as we rode from a hopeless case – stirred his mind – this man mark you was passively good – but had become almost a sceptic. In two months or three I stood by his bed side – his too a hopeless case. Weir had no cant – we prayed earnestly together – knowing he was dying, he assured us that he was convinced that heaven was his portion and I believe it – may you and I Kate die likewise – thankfully and in loving kindness will all

Yours truly,

H.H. RADCLIFFE

Henry's longing for a wife would ultimately be fulfilled but before that happened there was yet another gold rush and a further consignment of drugs from his brothers. Exactly when he moved to Inglewood is not known but he wrote to John from there on 20 November 1860:

Australia Victoria
Inglewood

My dear John,

P. Sandeman manager of the National Provincial Bank Lichfield is instructed by his mail to place to your credit the sum of sixty pounds £60..0..0 from Bradburne.

You must not be alarmed about the money for after I have received the goods now on the sea I shall not require to send to Melbourne which if it could have been prevented would have more than paid for the whole of the goods from England – I shall keep up the remittance of twenty pounds per month if however my business increases I shall add to the amount –

> Oct. 8th to 14th 21..3.00
> 15th to Nov. 5th 45..7..0
> to 12 28..5..0
> Nov. 18 38..18..3

I never expected that Inglewood would have continued this last month to pay me.

I have money sufficient to remove in the Bank but not to cover a loss from fire which is now a matter of dread –

Inglewood will be a permanent place in consequence of the extraordinary richness of our reefs they will last a few years but only employ a limited number of men. Bradburne is again a storekeeper in Inglewood and talks of taking a wife who he tells me has upward of £500 per annum.

I fully expected to hear of the miniatures but I fear you have neglected them – if they do not come with the next goods I shall have to wait for a long time for do not think I shall require goods for some time.

I am surprised to hear of Statham's misfortune – his son here is no credit I was determined not to pay Bradburne before I heard from you I pay him for his own orders and £1¾ per cent –

I am sorry to hear that Richard continues to borrow it is a bad game and must end in failure I do not consider that I do so – because I certainly pay fully half before I receive and could pay the whole if I only received stock from England however I shall be soon in advance.

My health continues good although I have denied myself proper hunting exercise to grub up a few fees.

I rode 44 miles in five hours last Monday week and returned in six hours with a rest of six hours – horse not distressed and no feed on the road – rode the same horse 120 miles in two spells in two nights and a day – weight about 14 st. Considering 60 miles without food at one time our horses must be good. I should have thought it killing horses in England to mount at 4 a.m. and remain in the seat to 6 p.m. with nothing to eat except a few mouthfuls of grass and water I have done this frequently for days together when hunting and a good colonial horse if he does not get galled will not knock-up.

Yours truly,

H.H. RADCLIFFE
To John Radcliffe Esq.

CHAPTER 8
Later Years

Henry's move to Inglewood was important inasmuch as it marked a change in his domestic situation: he got married. His wife whom he married in 1861 or 1862 was Charlotte Julia Fuller (sometimes Fullerton). She must have been sixteen or seventeen years old when they married: Henry was forty-two.

They had eight children. The first born, Alice Maud, did not live into adulthood and is probably buried at Inglewood. Subsequently they had: Bertha Charlotte (b. 1867), Emma Maud (b. *c.* 1869), Henry Hemmington (b. *c.*1870), Augusta Marion (b. *c.* 1872), John Frederick (b. *c.* 1873), Reginald (b. *c.* 1875) and Charles Frederick (b. *c.* 1876). A stillborn child was buried on 16 December 1876 in Ballarat.

Henry's hopes of a major gold find or a fortune as the owner of a drugstore in Inglewood were not realised. Some time prior to March 1868 he settled in Ballarat, then the largest and most permanent gold mining town in Victoria. He wrote a rather rambling letter to his eighteen-year-old nephew Harry (John's son) in March 1868 in which he says 'sometimes think of my dear Charlotte and old Pilgarlick'.

Ballarat in the early gold rush days was a dangerous place to be if you fell ill or suffered an injury. Many so-called doctors were quacks, and hospital treatment was almost unheard of. Prior to 1856 sick and injured people were housed in huts at the Government Camp. 'There were no hospitals or asylums in that early day, and a woman was an absolute phenomenon; so the sick man often died with nothing civilised about him but the awkward, if gentle, tending of his digging partners in the gold-hunting wilderness.'

Christmas Day 1855 saw the laying of the foundation stone of the first portion of Camp Hospital, but it only had four wards and was supposed to be limited to public servants. In 1860 it became the Ballarat District Hospital and subsequently it adopted its present title of the Ballarat Base Hospital. Further wings were added later in the 1860s. The Ballarat Benevolent Asylum was founded on St Patrick's Day 1859. It provided a home for aged and chronic invalids. In December 1869 there were 195 patients in the home. 'It is a palace in the Elizabethan style, with well-kept grounds, a magnificent home such as the English poor have never dreamt of in their wildest flights of fancy.'

We have read Henry's letter to Kate explaining his difficulties with the local doctors and his struggle, ultimately successful, to be recognised as a qualified doctor. As we know, he became a member of the Victoria Medical Board in September or October 1859.

When Henry settled in Ballarat in 1869 he had decided to revert to his old profession. That year (or possibly the next) he was appointed Honorary Surgical Officer at the District Hospital. He became Honorary Physician in 1873 and also Honorary Physician at the Benevolent Asylum. During the 1870s Henry was much involved in hospital politics. He was very alert to the risks of infection and worked tirelessly to instil a sense of awareness of cross-infection. By the 1880s he was probably concentrating on his private practice. In 1884 he only attended three General Committee Meetings (out of a possible sixteen) and failed to manage more than one House Committee meeting (out of a possible twenty-five). In 1885 Henry lost his post to the twenty-eight-year-old Stanislas Zichy-Woinaski, a Melbourne graduate, but the hospital benevolently (he was now about sixty-five) honoured him with the hospital's first consultant post. He became Honorary Consulting Physician. During the 1890s

Henry was active in promoting the nurses' training school and must have been gratified when four candidates passed the nurses' preliminary examination in 1891.

In 1894 Henry retired from the hospital but continued to practise privately. In his book *Medecine and Memories* (1960) D.W. Sloss says of Henry, 'He is supposed to have had a very lucrative practice. I called on him in 1902 and saw a very old, but very alert man.'

Henry died on 19 July 1903 and was buried in the Radcliffe grave at Ballarat Old Cemetery.

We can call it the Radcliffe grave because it had already been used several times to inter members of his family. His wife Charlotte, possibly exhausted by childbearing, died in Ballarat at the age of 44 in 1889. Their son Charles died in 1898 at the age of twenty-two. Two other children died young and were buried in the grave together with a stillborn baby. The grave is in a prominent position in Ballarat Old Cemetery, next to the Eureka Soldiers' memorial. It was restored in 1989 by Henry's great-granddaughter and the author.

Of Henry's family not a lot is known and what is established has mainly been gathered by word of mouth, as there is very little by way of letters or documents. His two eldest daughters, it would seem, never married and after Henry's death moved to Sydney. They, jointly, were the sole beneficiaries of Henry's will. He left realty not exceeding £600 and personalty not exceeding £400. His son, Henry Hemmington, was left nothing. Why this was so is not known. There may have been a rift between father and son. Henry Hemmington was sent to England as a young man with a view to becoming a solicitor, but he returned to Australia never having qualified, preferring Ballarat to Liverpool. He became the local cab proprietor and sometime undertaker. He lived in Raglan Street, a block distant from his father's house in Lyons Street

South, and the tale is that whenever he noticed his father going out on a call he would follow him in the hope that there might be a demise in the offing. This undoubtedly infuriated his father, which may explain the rift. Henry Hemmington married and had two daughters who both had families. He died in 1933 and was buried beside his father and mother. His younger sister Augusta Marion (known as Gussie or Daisy) settled back in England where she married a musician called Ernest Batten. They had a daughter, Kathleen. Daisy died in about 1950.

Henry's grave in Ballarat Old Cemetery is embellished with a brass plaque. Unfortunately, the family motto *'Virtus propter se'* ('Virtue is its own reward') is shown on the plaque as *'Virtus proper se'*. Nothing in Henry's life was totally perfect and so it was in death.

Bibliography

The World Rushed In by J. S. Holliday. Victor Gollancz Ltd., London, 1983.

One Man's Gold: The Letters & Journals of a Forty-Niner by Enos Christman, ed. Florence Morrow Christman. Whittlesey House, New York, 1930.

The Rush by Edward Dolnick. Little, Brown and Company, 2014.

Passage to America by Terry Coleman. Pimlico, 1972.

The Age of Gold by H. W. Brands. William Heinemann, London, 2005.

The Gold Rushes by W. P. Morrell. Adam & Charles Black, 1968 (2nd edition).

Historical Atlas of California by Warren A. Beck and Ynez D. Haase. University of Oklahoma Press, 1988 (6th printing).

Notes of Travel in California by Fremont & Emory. James M'Glashan, Dublin, 1849.

History of Ballarat by W. B. Withers. Ballarat Heritage Services, 1999.

A Mid-Californian Illustrated History by George Emanuels. Diablo Books, 1995.

An American Genocide by Benjamin Madley. Yale University Press, 2016.

Index

A

Ajax
   fellow passengers and crew, 16–17
   Henry's decision to embark on, 8, 12
   Henry's departure, 15
   sightings of land, 23–4
   Valparaiso, 20, 24–30
   weather and storms on the voyage, 17–23

Australia
   gold rush, 70, 74–9, 84, 93
   Henry as a druggist, 80–2, 84–5, 93
   Henry's gold prospecting in, 75–9, 84, 93
   Henry's medical accreditation in Australia, 82–3, 94
   Henry's medical practice, 79, 80, 86, 94–5
   Henry's move to, 10, 71, 72, 75
   Henry's precarious finances, 85
   Henry's views on, 86–7
   Inglewood, 90–1, 93
   wine production, 85–6

B

Ballarat, 9, 74–5, 76, 87, 93
Ballarat District Hospital, 94–5
Ballarat Old Cemetery, 95, 96
Beale, Tom, 16–17
Bear Flag Revolt, 57

C

California
    under American control, 55–8
    Bear Flag Revolt, 57
    Californians in England, 68–9
    Henry's departure, 70–1
    Henry's importation of merchandise, 32–3
    Henry's positive attitude towards, 52–3, 64–5, 66–9
    Henry's prospecting trips, 44–8, 55
    medical employment, 33, 35
    Vallejo, 66
    see also Native American population; San Francisco; Stockton
Christman, Enos, 38–40, 42–3
Clacy, Ellen, 83

D

Daily Alta California, 55

F

Forest Creek, Australia, 75–6, 83
Fremont, John Charles, 57–8

G

gold prospecting
    in Australia, 70, 74–9, 84, 93
    in Ballarat, 74–5, 76, 93
    gold fever in California, 14, 38
    Henry in Australia, 75–9, 84, 93
    Henry in California, 44–8, 55
    impact on the Native American population, 54, 58–9

in Mariposa, 36, 38, 58–9
  violent incidents, 49–50
Gunn, Dr Lewis C., 42

H
Harvey, Walter, 63
Higgins, Charles, 81

K
Kings River, 44

L
Larkin, Thomas, 58
Lindley, Emma, 48, 88
Liverpool Workhouse, 12
Long, James, 10, 12, 48

M
Mariposa, California
  gold prospecting, 36, 38, 59
    Henry's financial losses, 44–5, 64
    Henry's medical practice, 52
    Henry's prospecting in, 44, 47
Mariposa War, 59–61
Marvin, J.G., 41, 42, 62–3
Mexican–American War, 56
Moore, Thomas, 'As Slow Our Ship,' 16 n1
Mount Alexander (Castlemaine), 76, 77

N

Native American population
   employed in James Savage's prospecting business, 58–9
   gold prospecting's impact on, 54, 58–9
   James Savage and the Tularenos, 58, 61–2, 63
   Mariposa War, 59–62
   settlers' attitudes towards, 54–5

O

Ovens River, Australia, 75–6, 78

R

Radcliffe, Charles, 8
Radcliffe, Charlotte Julia (née Fuller), 92, 95
Radcliffe, Emma (née Hughes), 8
Radcliffe, George
   Henry's encouragement to, 12–13
   lack of industry, 12, 28–9
   mental health, 8–9, 69
Radcliffe, Henry
   affection for Kate, 8, 14
   as associate Judge of Tuolumne City, 37, 48
   attitude towards the Native American population, 54, 55
   burial in Ballarat Old Cemetery, 95, 96
   Californian property, 65–6
   career as a druggist, 80–2, 84–5, 93
   children, 9, 93, 95–6
   contact with his family in England, 9, 69–70, 72–4
   death, 87, 95, 96
   dogs, 87–8

    family background, 7–9, 10
    finances, 11–12
    food provisions, 15, 18, 26, 35
    horse trading in Australia, 76, 78–9, 92
    ill health, 47–8, 64, 65
    letter-writing, 10
    marriage to Charlotte Fuller, 92, 95
    medical accreditation in Australia, 82–3, 94
    medical employment, 11, 13, 33, 35, 43, 49–53, 71, 75, 79, 80, 86, 94–5
    medical training, 10–11
    as a newspaper man, 35–44
    pharmaceutical supplies from England, 81–2, 84–5, 90–1
    positive attitude towards California, 52–3, 64–5, 66–9
    religious beliefs, 8, 27, 48–9
    social life, 11, 39, 48
    in Stockton, 34, 35–53
    surgical skills, 50–2
    thoughts on marriage, 88–9
Radcliffe, Henry Hemmington, 9, 10, 93, 95–6
Radcliffe, Irene, 9
Radcliffe, John (brother)
    care for George Radcliffe, 69
    children, 29
    drugs sent to Henry, 81–2, 84–5, 90–1
    Henry's close relationship with, 10
    Henry's departure, 15
    Henry's medical accreditation in Australia, 84
    marriage to Emma Hughes, 8
    marriage to Kate, 8, 14, 29–30

   pharmaceutical supplies to Henry, 90–2
Radcliffe, John (grandfather), 7
Radcliffe, Kate, 8, 15, 29–30, 36, 52, 66–7, 73–4, 87–90
Radcliffe, Mary Anne (née Hayton) (mother), 7–8, 9, 29, 69
Radcliffe, Mary Anne (sister), 9, 29, 69
Radcliffe, Reginald, 8, 10, 69
   pharmaceutical supplies to Henry, 81–2, 84–5, 90–1
   religious beliefs, 27, 48–9
Radcliffe, Richard (brother), 8, 10, 15, 27–8
Radcliffe, Richard (father), 7–8, 9, 10
Ramage presses, 35, 37, 40–1
Reynolds, Judge James R., 41–2
Robb, John, 43

S

San Francisco
   as a boom town, 28, 31–2, 34
   California years, 35
   fires, 70
   Henry's antipathy towards, 33, 36
   Henry's arrival in, 30–1, 56
   Henry's hopes of selling imported goods, 30, 32–3
   Henry's medical practice, 52–3
   port, 14, 30
Savage, James D.
   in the California Battalion, 57
   employment of Native Americans for gold prospecting, 58–9, 60–2
   Mariposa War, 59–62
   murder, 62–3
   and the Tularenos (Southern Yokut) Indians, 58, 61–2, 63

Sonora, California, 37–8
Sonora Herald
   Enos Christman as the typesetter for, 40–1, 42–3
   funding for, 41–2, 44
   Henry's founding of, 37–8
Stockton
   fires, 47, 52–3, 70
   Henry as a newspaper man, 35–44
   Henry's medical practice, 43, 49–52, 71
   Methodist Church, 49
Stockton Hospital, 44, 50, 71
Stockton Journal, 43
Stockton Times (and Tuolumne City Intelligencer)
   advert for Henry's medical practice, 49
   attitude towards the Native American population, 54–5
   Enos Christman as the typesetter for, 39–40
   Henry's founding of, 35–7, 71
   Ramage press, 35, 37, 40–1
   valedictory edition, 43–4

T
Tularenos (Southern Yokut) Indians, 58
Tuolumne City, 36–7, 48, 65

V
Vallejo, California, 66
Vallejo, Mariano, 66

W
White, John, 36–7, 41, 42, 50, 55